DEDICATION:

Thank you doesn't express our thoughts fully. We have found that words aren't enough to explain the amount of love and support we have felt over the last 3 years especially. After putting together this book, we realize there are many other people that aren't even talked about within these pages that supported us through prayers, visits, text messages, money, and list goes on. We love and appreciate you so much. This book is dedicated to you all.

"I thank my God in all my remembrance of you, always offering prayer with joy in my every prayer for you all, in view of your participation in the gospel from the first day until now." - Philippians 1:3-5

INTRODUCTION – Rob Futral, Pastor

Love never fails. Those three Spirit-inspired words have settled deep into many hearts long after they soaked a parchment page. Written by the Apostle Paul to a community of Christ-followers who were seeking the Lord's way even as they struggled along theirs, he wrote to reinforce what they believed, what they had experienced, and what they had declared as their own. Love never fails.

That truth is tested in our lives every day in small and often significant ways. Then come the moments that seem to shake everything we know, everything we trust, and everything we have believed. We wonder if those three simple words hold true. So we press and pull, strain, and struggle with this truth, waiting for it to be proven false and for it to crack like a flimsy foundation. But it doesn't. It holds like an anchor wedged into a gigantic granite slab that is unmovable.

The story you are about to read is an amazing illustration of this truth. The people you will read about are ordinary people with an extraordinary God who have lived in and lived out their faith through a challenging journey. I say that because you will be tempted to say, "those people are superhuman and superheroes!" They are indeed "Greenwood Strong", but that strength comes from their Source-the Great Shepherd and Savior of their souls-Jesus Christ. They share their story with you so that you can find the same Source in your own unfolding story. As their pastor, I have been privileged to walk some of their paths with them. I can tell you that what they share they have lived and are living.

I can also tell you that they want you to experience what they have experienced. I know that from personal experience. So whoever you are, wherever you are, and whatever you are going through, start reading and be reminded: Love never fails.

The beginning of the journey

We didn't realize that this Facebook post would begin the new journey we would be facing:

We received many comments on this Facebook post from people who seemed to have similar experiences and who received relief from going to physical therapists to people who had to have back surgery. Several comments asked if he had been sitting on his wallet. And, we thought...yes, he does do that! So he switched it to his front pocket. One comment seemed to be more urgent, "Go to the doctor!" But, at the time, in the sea of the other comments, it only stands out now to us. Another comment from a family friend, Jannifer, also stands out. Many people said that they were praying for Roosevelt, but as we read her comment now, oh, how we would need these specific prayers so much in the days coming. She wrote, "

Lord, touch my brother. He has too much work to do to be held captive to this temporary issue! Remember his faithfulness! Let The Blood Cover! Be healed! Be delivered! Be set free! It is so." She concluded it with a picture of a blood drop. We thank God for the blood shed by Jesus to save us from our sins, but also to help us in our time of trouble.

1 Peter 2:24 – He himself bore our sins in his body on the cross, so that we might die to sins and live for righteousness; by his wounds you have been healed.

Go to the doctor, friends!! Whatever your ailment...just go to the doctor. It's better to be safe and find out what's truly going on. We are so thankful for the day that we worked out together. He wouldn't have been doing leg extensions if we weren't together, and because he was maybe showing off just a little, he had more weight than he needed. Doesn't every man show off for the woman that he loves and wants to impress? I'm so thankful that he loved me enough to show off his strength. That kind of love would take us through the coming days, weeks, and years. We had no idea that it would be cancer.

We are telling our story because we felt that it was never ours in the first place. The following posts, chronicle our journey through Facebook updates and reflections. We pray that through our journey one person's life will be changed.

This was the week after Roosevelt's first chemo treatment at Chelsey & Brad's wedding. The family from left to right: Noah, 16, Chandler, 18, Adam 7, Shay & Roosevelt, Bria, 20, and Jacob, 14.

The day of his diagnosis. Roosevelt getting his vitals checked by Teri, our friend, and hospital doctor.

The Diagnosis of Stage 4 Metastatic Prostate Cancer –

John 16:33 says, "In this world, you will have trouble...", and it's amazing how it doesn't resonate with you until you have trouble. Not that we haven't experienced trouble in our lives: you just don't think about it too much until it happens. I have read it over and over again and really wasn't immune to trouble in my life. But, on September 7, 2016, at around 4:30p.m., trouble totally engulfed and overwhelmed us. Our friend Teri, who was the doctor on call that day, sat down on the hospital bed with me sitting across from her on the hospital couch and said, "Shay...Roosevelt has cancer." My heart was absolutely crushed. I don't really even like to relive that day because the emotions are so deep. Even now, my heart palpitates, I get a lump in my throat, and tears consume my eyes as I think about the forever moment that changed our lives.

How can this be my life now?

How could this happen?

We are doing everything we can to live for You, Lord!

Isn't that such a normal thought??

I literally started crying out to God as soon as I heard her say, "...he has cancer"...Father, in the name of Jesus...we thank you for being our Father...we thank you for a Sovereign God who knows and sees all... Even though I don't remember my exact words, I just remember saying to God, Thank you...thank you...thank you...

I knew down deep in my soul that the Lord still sits on the throne of our life no matter the circumstances, even though my head wasn't there yet.

Roosevelt had been given medication because of the tremendous pain he was in, but as soon as I started crying out to God about the news, he woke up, and I started hugging him and crying while still praying out loud.

I'm sure Teri has had to give that same diagnosis time and again. I can't imagine how she must have felt having to be the bearer of bad news to friends.

There are so many words that can describe hearing a cancer diagnosis about someone you love. We were devastated, perplexed, and in utter disbelief. In that moment, all the emotions from ALL the trouble we have ever experienced started flooding back. I was already a little irritated about all the other "cancers" in our married life: two pregnancy losses, loss of a job, loss of a dream home, loss of relationships, loss of our pastor (my father-in-law) and mother-in-law to cancer, and disappointments that come with being an entrepreneur. I was basically just trying to "suck it up" and keep going. My life wasn't turning out like I thought it would. Because of the trouble, I was developing a little chip on my shoulder. I knew I was going down this road of being a Woman Martyr – You know who that is, right? It's a woman who thinks that she does everything right and everyone does everything wrong. She's the woman who does everything for everyone else in her immediate family, but no one seems to do anything right for her. She is the type of woman who feels alone in her household because it's just assumed that she is fine and strong enough to handle whatever comes her way, so no one stops to ask her, "Are you okay?" You know that woman: you may be her or know someone like her. I hope that I'm not alone in this thought.

Three weeks before this, Roosevelt had a weight lifting injury (or so we thought). How I now wish that was all he had. We were working out together at the gym. While doing the leg extension machine, Roosevelt wondered why the left leg couldn't lift the same weight as the right leg, so he forced it up. He knew something didn't feel right, but, he didn't know why. The next day, he felt pain going down his left leg into his foot, and as the days went on, the more pain he felt. We asked our Facebook friends (because they have all the answers!) and everyone we knew what they thought may be wrong with him based upon his symptoms. They thought maybe he sat too long on a trip to Dallas, TX, and maybe he shouldn't be sitting with his wallet in his back pocket. Maybe it was Sciatic nerve pain, which can radiate from your spine into your leg. Over the counter medicines weren't working to decrease the pain, and, honestly, I was irritated. I was irritated because this busy momma of 5 children and a busy entrepreneur had no time for my husband to be sick, and seriously, the pain cannot be that bad, right? (Can you see my head and eyes rolling saying...Ain't nobody got time for this!) If you are a woman, you know exactly what I'm talking about! I even said it to him. He went to the chiropractor for 2 weeks, and I said to myself, "I don't have time to go with him," so I didn't. He would come home each day with no real progress. After 2 weeks, I said to him that it doesn't look like you are getting better. He came home the next week, and the chiropractor suggested that he should get an MRI.

The next week, I asked him if he had scheduled an MRI. He told me that he had not.

"Don't you think you need to get one?" I asked, in an irritated tone.

We called our friend Teri who is a Hospitalist at a local hospital, and she had someone at a local facility call with an MRI appointment for 6 weeks later. I knew in my heart that there was no way that he could wait that long. The pain seemed to be getting worse day by day. Roosevelt had even started sleeping on the floor to get a little relief with no success. Remember, this busy momma didn't have time for it . I called Teri back and explained that the facility was talking about scheduling an MRI for 6 weeks later. She said that she would admit him into the hospital to get the MRI done faster. So, we scheduled him to be admitted into the hospital on Wednesday Sept 7th, 2016, after four weeks with no relief from the pain that he was feeling. We decided that I would meet him at the hospital after a bible study class that I taught at Ballet Magnificat for the ballet training program that my daughter was involved in at the time. Remember, this busy momma had no time to take him to an appointment because I just couldn't add one more thing to my plate. And, besides, the pain can't be that bad, right?

At this time, we thought the worse case scenario would be a pinched nerve or a herniated disc that may need back surgery. We NEVER thought anything else could be wrong with him. Nothing. After Bible study, I showed up in his hospital room, and he was asleep. He said that the pain was still severe, and I thought, "why would they still have him in pain?" Really? I thought he would be resting with prescription-strength medicine by this time. They gave him Dilaudid which is supposed to be more potent than morphine. They gave him another shot after I asked about it, and he drifted off to sleep. I sat there and waited, so thankful that we were there to get him the help that he really needed, especially after weeks of the chiropractor working on him without any real answers.

Just then, Teri came in and gave us the real reason for his pain.

At this point, that busy momma chip on my shoulder fell away.

My heart melted for my husband in that instant that she uttered the words, "Shay, Roosevelt has cancer." I hugged him, feeling so badly for my lack of empathy for his pain.

I also felt sorry for all the times that I thought that he should "suck it up" or "man up".

Just in case this ever happens to you, or if you have gone through this as a wife, you should understand that these feelings are normal and God gives you grace to get over your guilt.

This story is for anyone who has had cancer or loved someone with cancer. Even if it wasn't the disease itself, everyone has some sort of 'cancer' in their life at some point.

This is our story about the one "cancer" in our life that we had to cling to our relationship with the Lord with every fiber of our being.

We want you to know that whatever cancer you are fighting that your brothers and sisters have gone through the same. Scripture says: But resist him, firm in your faith, knowing that the same experiences of suffering are being accomplished by your brethren who are in the world (1 Peter 5:9).

Once I stopped praying, I looked and Teri was sitting there. I think I remember her saying what the next steps would be for that week. Honestly, I don't remember her exact words. Things started happening fast. Yet I felt strong and capable.

Roosevelt and I hugged and cried, and he kept saying that he was sorry.

Hearing him say that he was sorry made me so sad.

It made me feel like this was the beginning of the end.

Of course, because of his parents dying from cancer, we couldn't help but think that cancer equaled death. In my mind, it did. I had an uncle whom I was very close to die from pancreatic cancer when I was a freshman in college, just 6 months after his diagnosis.

"Everyone dies of cancer at some point," I thought to myself.

"What am I going to do without him?" the thoughts continued.

I felt that I was losing the husband who God gave us to provide for us, protect us, make us laugh, and give us wisdom.

My next thoughts were about our children. What are we going to tell them?

How are we going to tell them this devastating news?

At this time, Noah was 16, Jacob was turning 15 in 5 days, and Adam was 5.

Bria, 20 years old, was driving back home from a local ballet studio after training all day, and, Chandler, 18 years old , was just 30 minutes away at Mississippi

College in Clinton, MS. We found out later that she was at our church, Broadmoor Baptist Church in Madison, at a worship rehearsal.

Whom should we call? Whom DO you call first?

And, how are we going to not have it be on social media until we can tell everyone who needed to know from us?

We knew that we couldn't tell the kids over the phone. We called Bria and asked her to bring the boys to the hospital. Next, we called Chandler and asked her if she could come to the hospital. I think we even said, "Everything is okay. We just need for you to come here." My stomach aches to even write these words remembering how to tell them horrible news. Insert screaming and crying in my heart here. There is nothing like going through something this difficult. I immediately felt strong for Roosevelt and strong for the kids. I had to. I didn't feel like I had a choice.

The kids finally got there. I can't even remember how we said it or what we said.

I do remember everyone hugging and crying.

Later I called my sister and mom on 3-way. I remember standing in the hallway looking out the window of the hospital, wishing none of this was true.

I think we then called Roosevelt's family, close friends, and church members.

We asked to say anything until we could tell who we needed to tell.

From there, everyone called each other. Everything really runs together from that night.

I do remember the kids wanting to tell their friends and post it on social media.

For some reason, we didn't hesitate letting them do that. I think at that point, we just wanted everyone to connect with whomever they felt like they needed to connect with to feel normal, and I'm so thankful for that. I'm thankful for the openness God gave to us to share because the immediate support and prayers we received from SO many people still resonate with our family even today. We will spend the rest of our lives trying to pay forward every meal, every dollar, every act of kindness, every prayer, every encouraging word to others that need it. Saying thank you to the amazing people we know and don't know will never be enough. We wish that we could remember every single name to thank. Just know that we love and appreciate you!

Shay Greenwood updated her status.
September 8, 2016 · 🌐

‹   …

Pray for our family especially my husband...**Roosevelt Greenwood** has prostate cancer.
He has a bone biopsy in the morning because they found malignancy on his spine and that will give us more news. (That's why he was having the nerve pain recently that we thought was a weight lifting injury.)
That sounds so dry and unemotional.
But it's just the truth.
It's the truth about life.
It gives you circumstances that are totally outside of your control that make you mad and numb. And, what do we do with it?
We lay it at God's feet...the feet of Jesus.
Why?
Because all you have to hold onto is your faith and the Creator who knew us before the foundation of the world...who holds the moon, sun, stars in the sky. Who knows every hair on your head? Who sees all and knows all? Who is all-powerful, all-knowing, all sufficient...and he cares about little ole you and me. He knows everything about what we are going through and we can trust Him with it all. I type all of that to not put on some kind of act of faith...or faking like I believe...it's because I believe all of that with every fiber of my being and nothing changes that even now.

Satan comes to kill steal and destroy...but we have a God that is greater no matter what things look like. Jesus said to Peter that Satan has demanded to sift you like wheat, but I've prayed for you that your faith would not fail.

And it's not. Pray that the Lord provides the doctor's immediate wisdom in this...his biopsy is in the morning. It's been a tough day for us. Pray we can sleep. We appreciate your prayers and Roosevelt does too because he keeps asking me...did you tell your FB friends to pray yet? He knows that prayer warriors make a difference. Thank you for all of you who have already prayed, texted, or came by...we love you BIG!
#godhasthis
#roosevelt greenwood
#greenwoodstrong
Bria Greenwood
Chandler Greenwood
Noah Javon Greenwood
Jacob Greenwood

👍 Like   💬 Comment   ↪ Share

😮😢😮 Michelle Mimi Davis and 516 others

222 shares

Roosevelt's Reflection:

Is this real?

I can't believe this is real.

I'm too young to have this happen to me.

I have a wife and 5 beautiful children.

And I have failed them.

How can one be in so much pain, but prior to the pain have no symptoms...none....zero??

I had excruciating pain...I couldn't even walk two steps without having to sit down.

The pain was so severe, that I was doing everything in my power to relieve myself of the pain. I took Tylenol, Advil, Aleve, and muscle relaxers and nothing was touching the pain. Hot baths and showers would give me a little relief, but then I was back to a level 10 pain in my back. On the rare occasion that I did sleep, I would go to sleep with the pain and wake up with the pain. I've never have felt pain like this in all my life.

In my mind, I thought something was sitting on a nerve, and I needed more relief than the chiropractor to find out what was causing me all the pain I was in. Never one time did I think that Teri would tell us that I had cancer. And not only did I have cancer, but it was at Stage 4. What I know about Stage 4 cancer is that it means death.

Am I going to die? I don't want to die. I'm ready... I mean I am a Christian, so I will get to live with Jesus, but I have a wife and 5 children. Who is going to take care of them? My children aren't married yet, I don't have grandchildren, and I have a 5 year old. This can't be how my life ends.

I don't remember a lot about these first days after the diagnosis – I remember being in a lot of pain. I remember being sad. I remember a lot of people coming in and out of the hospital. I remember people coming and praying for me. And, I remember being very emotional. I'm still full of emotions about what I go through on a daily basis and what my future holds.

Shay's Reflection:

I remember immediately googling everything that I could about Prostate cancer. I knew that he would have a biopsy in the morning to rule out any other cancers. I already knew that I needed to ask for prayer for sleep. How can anyone sleep with news like this? We were so thankful for so many people coming to our rescue. We had so many people thinking for us, doing things for us, all without asking. They just knew that we would need certain things, like they had already walked down this road before. I was overwhelmed and overloaded with so many thoughts, and was so amazed at the love we felt. One vivid call came from a church friend, who called and said, "I'm on the way to the grocery store, and I need to have a list of things your kids will eat. We are having a freezer delivered to your house today." We had so many friends bring us things to ease our hospital stay as well: money, snacks, and so many people who came by to specifically pray for Roosevelt, for me, and for our family. There is nothing like having this kind of support when you are going through a tragic event. I felt more and more overwhelmed by the day. It was nice to have just us in the room after a day of visitors who were as devastated as we were.

As I look back on the beginning of this...the best thing we did was to be vulnerable and reach out and tell anyone and everyone what we were going through. Friends and family can heal hearts and ease the difficulty of hard situations.

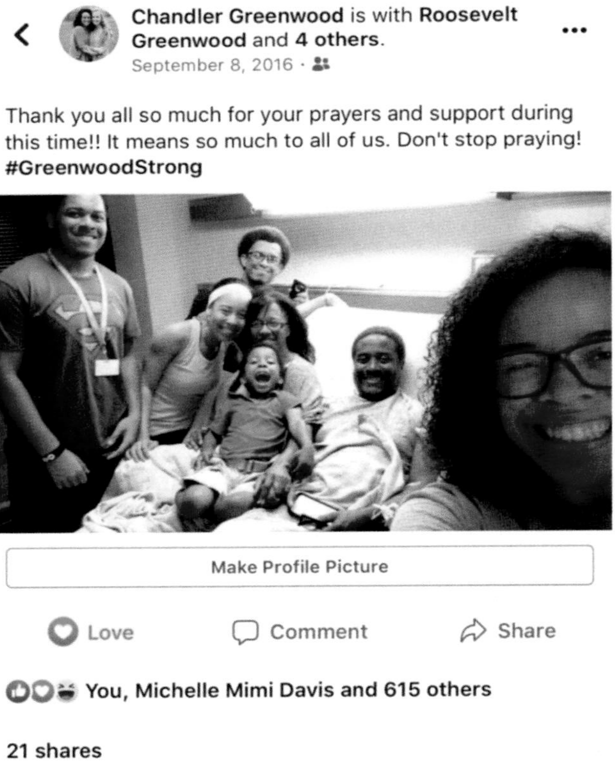
Chandler Greenwood is with Roosevelt Greenwood and 4 others.
September 8, 2016 ·
Thank you all so much for your prayers and support during this time!! It means so much to all of us. Don't stop praying! #GreenwoodStrong
Make Profile Picture
Love
Comment
Share
You, Michelle Mimi Davis and 615 others
21 shares

Chandler's Perspective (2nd born daughter to Roosevelt & Shay, 18 years old at diagnosis)

It was a Wednesday night that I will never forget. I was in band rehearsal (I was scheduled to lead worship that night in my youth group at church) when I received a phone call from my dad. He called once, and I let it go to voicemail because the band was in the middle of soundcheck for the night. I knew that my dad was going to the hospital to get an MRI on his back because of the constant pain he was in (he could barely walk), so I knew that he was probably just calling to tell me the results of his MRI. I told myself that I would just call him after rehearsal was over. After the first call from him went through, it was not long before he started calling me again. I knew then that I needed to answer the phone because it's not like my dad to call twice in a row, especially because he knew I was at church and in rehearsal. So I took a step away from rehearsal into one of the side rooms to answer the phone. I answered the phone and my dad's first words were calmly, "Hey Chandler, can you come down to the hospital?" Really confused, I said, "Hey Dad, I'm in band rehearsal right now..can I come tonight after church? What's up?" He didn't answer my question and asked me again if I could come up to the hospital. I said, "Do you need me to? What's going on?" He told me that everything was fine, but that he needed me to come to the hospital. Wanting a direct answer, I said, "Dad. You're scaring me. What's wrong? Is everything okay?" My dad then broke down into tears and passed the phone to my mom and said, "Here, Shay." I knew then that there was something seriously wrong, I just didn't know what. I went through a list of things it could be in my head, but never once did I think about cancer. My mom got on the phone and said, "Hey, honey, can you come to the hospital?" I then asked her if everything was okay and what was going on, and she would not give me a direct answer, either. Worried almost to frustration because they didn't give me any answers over the phone, I told her that I would be there as soon as I could. So I then went back into the main room where the band was rehearsing, and I said to the worship leader in charge, "Hey Ricky, my dad is in the hospital, and he just asked me to come up to the hospital." He looked at me with concern in his eyes, and simply said, "Go!". So then I packed up my stuff as fast as I could and took off running for my car.

Shaking with worry, anxiety, and fear, I hopped in my car, turned on my hazard lights and drove as fast as could (while still being in control) to the hospital. On my way there I began to pray and tell the Lord that I didn't know what was going on, but that I wanted Him to heal my dad in whatever he was going through. The Lord began to remind me in that moment that, no matter what I face in this life, I can still say, "it is well," simply because of who He is. The worry, anxiety, and fear that I experienced upon arriving to my car slowly began to fade away as I immediately began to experience the peace of God that surpasses all understanding start to guard my heart and my mind in Christ Jesus (Philippians 4:7). I had grown up my whole life hearing this verse, but right then and there was the first time I had actually experienced the peace of God for myself. And Scripture is right—it truly does surpass all understanding! There was no explaining this peace I had other than it was completely Jesus.

After a 15 minute drive, I finally arrived at the hospital (I was the first to arrive out of my four other siblings). I began to well up with tears and choked over my words as I began to ask the receptionist where my dad was. She told me what his room number was, I thanked her, and then booked it to the room as fast as I could. I arrived to the room, and the door was open. My mom was on the phone, and my dad was sitting on the hospital bed with a blank, distraught look on his face. With my heart pounding, I asked them what was wrong. Silence. My Dad patted a spot on the bed beside him so that I could come and sit beside him. I sat beside him on the bed and then he began to muster up the words that would end up shaking my world.

"I have cancer," my dad said. I can still remember the look on his face as he told me. He was devastated. I was devastated. "What? How?" I asked. My dad then took me in his arms and held me as we began to weep together. I began thinking to myself, "How in the world could this happen?! No, not cancer. Why my dad? Why our family?" Never in a million years would I ever even think that cancer would be a part of my immediate family's story. But now, it is.

It's in moments like these where my family and I had to ask ourselves, "do we really believe what we say we believe?" That Jesus is good? (Psalm 34:8) That He is for us? (Romans 8:31) That He sees us? (Proverbs 5:21) That He is our refuge and strength? (Psalm 46:1) That He's with us? (Joshua 1:9) That He's fighting for us? (Exodus 14:14)

How can we say that? How can my family and I say that Jesus is good when we have been dealt with life altering circumstances that have shaken us to our core and changed our world forever? Well, we can say that He is good simply because He is. We say it by faith. For, "now faith is confidence in what we hope for and assurance about what we do not see," Hebrews 11:1. We rest in His promises. We take Him at His Word. We remember all that He's done for us. And then we praise Him for what He has already done and all that He is going to do! As my dad always says, "in the end, we win." Thank YOU, Jesus! We can say that He is good because He has proven His goodness and faithfulness to us time and time again, and, something that we have learned as a family is that it's okay to know these truths and be sad, all at the same time.

My eyes just popped open and I looked over at the hospital bed and thought to myself, "Oh, God, that's right, my husband has cancer." I had absolutely no tears last night before going to bed. But then, the reality punches you in the stomach all over again, friends. It is more than you can take. People say all the time..."God won't put more on you than you can bare." That's not true. Oh, Yes, He will. It's unbearable. Until then you take your thoughts captive and remember, that your relationship with an all-powerful God makes it bearable. The situation takes your breath, you can't even catch your breath. And then you cry out to God knowing that He has every breath you need. We cannot make it without having a personal relationship with Jesus Christ. And I don't want to.

Cancer is NOT an automatic death sentence. You know that, right? We find security when we trust in the Lord...

Psalm 91
He who dwells in the shelter of the Most High
Will abide in the shadow of the Almighty.
2 I will say to the Lord, "My refuge and my fortress,
My God, in whom I trust!"
3 For it is He who delivers you from the snare of the trapper
And from the deadly pestilence.
4 He will cover you with His pinions,
And under His wings you may seek refuge;
His faithfulness is a shield and bulwark.
5 You will not be afraid of the terror by night,
Or of the arrow that flies by day;
6 Of the pestilence that [a]stalks in darkness,
Or of the destruction that lays waste at noon.
7 A thousand may fall at your side
And ten thousand at your right hand,
But it shall not approach you.
8 You will only look on with your eyes
And see the recompense of the wicked.
9 For you have made the Lord, my refuge,
Even the Most High, your dwelling place.
10 No evil will befall you,
Nor will any plague come near your tent.
11 For He will give His angels charge concerning you,
To guard you in all your ways.
12 They will bear you up in their hands,
That you do not strike your foot against a stone.
13 You will tread upon the lion and cobra,

The young lion and the serpent you will trample down.
14 "Because he has loved Me, therefore I will deliver him;
I will set him securely on high, because he has known My name.
15 "He will call upon Me, and I will answer him;
I will be with him in trouble;
I will rescue him and honor him.
16 "With a long life I will satisfy him
And let him see My salvation."

Our family took a picture last night from the hospital bed. The kids wanted to put it on their snapchat. And I thought to myself...of course, they do and of course they can. We should live our lives out loud, for all to see as a testament to the glory of the Lord. That's just what we do. What are we going to call the picture?? (Because that's what you do in this social media age. You decide on a caption.) We were brainstorming captions...then we came up with the hashtag **#GreenwoodStrong**. Because we are. We are Greenwoods. And we are strong. ...We are stronger together.

This family has never done anything small. You already know that. We do things BIG. We go Big, or we go home. We do big things like living through a tornado, miscarriages, having lots of children, homeschooling, quitting a corporate job, losing a job, losing a dream home, and now cancer. Did you know that normal psa levels for your prostate are 4 or below? Roosevelt's is at 1490!!! The decimal comes after the zero. We had no symptoms before this. Because, we do BIG things around here. God has called us to do big things in this family. Nooooo, not small things! (Say that last sentence with a sarcastic tone) Big, gigantic, enormous things that are so incredibly unbelievable that you are like....How in the world did I get here?! How do you get here without symptoms? ...And then you remember....you are #Greenwoodstrong....you are called to great big things....because you have a great big God that as He takes you through it that He will receive all the glory when He shows the miraculous through it.
So get ready!! It going to be a battle. And we are so grateful that you are going to fight it with us. We are more than overwhelmed by our family and friends. The things you have done already for this family are just too much to take. There are no words...it's a love that totally engulfs you. It's a kind of love that our pastor said as we prayed in the hospital that if "love could heal, Roosevelt would be healed instantly today". What a blessing you are! I have read every message and if I haven't responded yet. I plan to. Keep praying! We will need those prayers. We love all of you!

Roosevelt's reflection:

In the middle of the night, I was lying there and I couldn't sleep, although they had given me sleep aids. I wanted to sleep because I didn't want all these thoughts running through my head. I was thinking that maybe if they gave me more meds to help me sleep, I could just sleep on and not have to deal with any of this. I have stage 4 cancer. I can walk, talk, feed and bath myself, but I don't want to be a burden to my beautiful wife Shay. It would be easier to just die now in my sleep. As the night went on, I felt like I could easily go to sleep, but I heard Shay crying. Hearing her cry broke my heart. I started praying silently, "Lord, please help Shay. Give her a peace that surpasses her understanding, please Lord I don't want her to be sad, can you take the sadness away." I asked her to come and sleep next to me in the hospital bed. I held her until she fell asleep.

Shay's Reflection:

"If love could heal, Roosevelt would be healed already." prayed Rob Futral. He was our pastor at the time. Such powerful words.

Love heals. In Roosevelt's case, we knew that the love of God would heal him here on earth, or the love of God would take him home to Heaven to be with Jesus.

The love of God overwhelms. We have felt that over the past couple of years especially after this diagnosis. And it truly gave us a glimpse of how much love God had to have to give up His son Jesus to save us from our sins and to prove His righteousness. Did you know, "For God so loved the world that he gave His only begotten Son that whoever shall believe in Him shall not perish but have everlasting life?" John 3:16. It's amazing how going through this suffering allowed us to feel God's love more than we ever had before. Hard...and, yes, the situation sucks...no wonder Jesus said "Why have you forsaken me, Lord?" We definitely have felt those forsaken moments, but at the same time, knew that God hadn't left us at all - that His love and presence are always there.

Shay Greenwood was live.
September 12, 2016 · 🌐

...

#greenwoodstrong

16.9K Views

👍 Like   💬 Comment   ↗ Share

👍 Roosevelt Greenwood and 465 others

199 shares

Roosevelt's Reflection:

I felt overwhelmed by the love of everyone while we were in the hospital, and I had never really done a Facebook live video before, but I wanted to do one to thank everyone for praying. Most of the time, you never know who truly loves you, minus your immediate family and friends. There was such an outpouring of prayers and messages that really lifted my spirit at a time when I needed it most.

I am so thankful for a wife that gets all the details because all I remember was that they were letting me go home. Then, I got this fever, and she explained to me that I had to go back to the hospital and be readmitted. I was so very disappointed because it was my son's birthday and he had a football game. Through all of the extra's, I was excited about watching him play.

Shay's Reflection:

Roosevelt wanted to be able to say thank you to the many Facebook friends and family who had already been reaching out to him. He had gotten out of the hospital, and we were on our way to see the radiologist to talk about the next steps for radiation to his spine. Because I'm an overachiever, I packed all the things I felt we needed for the doctor's appointments and treatments. Snacks, a book, and my calendar, just to name a few. The night before, Roosevelt had a slight fever, and I called the doctor as I was instructed to do because he just had the prostate biopsy a few days before. They told me to give him ibuprofen and monitor him for the next 24 hours. God had me stick a thermometer in my purse on the way to the appointment. They emphasized that if Roosevelt contracted a fever, we needed to go back to the hospital. As we sat and waited for them to call us back for his radiology appointment, he felt warm, so I checked his temperature. It was 101 degrees. I couldn't believe it. I remember what they said and called the urologist, who conducted the biopsy. They said to bring him back to the hospital right then and that he would have to be admitted into the hospital. It was SO disappointing, because he was just discharged after being in the hospital for 5 days. It was also Jacob's birthday, and he was playing in a football game that night. Our hearts were broken, but we knew we had to pay attention to Roosevelt's health and do what the doctors said to do. The journey felt hard already and so out of our hands at this point. I kept saying to myself, though, that "it's all in God's hands."

We started calling all of our friends and family to let them know. Jacob had a junior varsity game that night that Roosevelt was super excited about and devastated that he couldn't go to now. He begged for me to not take him to the hospital and there was NO way that was happening. I made a commitment to take care of him the best way I knew how, and I knew that I was going to have to put my foot down to him no matter. Our sweet friend, Amber, bought a cookie cake and pizza for Jacob for his birthday, and we celebrated his birthday after the game in the hospital that night. We were holding on tightly to each other and for the times that we could have together, even though we were sad at the same time.

The kids went home that night and Roosevelt and I were once again in the hospital on our own. We were holding on to our faith knowing that it was all we could control at the time!! For God hath not given us the spirit of fear; but of power, and of love, and of a sound mind. 2 Timothy 1: 7

Shay Greenwood
September 13, 2016 · 🌐

I've been telling people that I need to shout from the roof tops how important it is for men to invest in their families...their wife #1 and their children #2...everyone else after that. God calls them to that...but, practically, there may come a day where someone has to take care of you. It is my pleasure to take care of this man because of the unconditional, sacrificial care and love he has always had for us. I know it's going to be hard, but I can do it without holding a grudge or being disrespectful, full of love in my heart. Why? Because he has made deposits into my heart and the hearts of his children. It's easy to give back.

Men...what are you doing to spend time loving on your wife and your children in ways that mean something to THEM? How are you caring for them?

Roosevelt is feeling good! We feel your prayers and know that there is a long road ahead of us. Keep praying! We both had the opportunity to talk to 2 nurses today one dating, the other getting married. What a joy to minister to them about relationships. I suggested "Love and Respect" by Emerson Eggerichs. Have you read it?! It may help you in your marriage. Could be an instant game changer for you. We love and appreciate all of you. 🖤🖤

#rooseveltgreenwood
#greenwoodstrong

👍 Like   💬 Comment   ↗ Share

👍😮 **Michelle Mimi Davis and 594 others**

33 shares

Roosevelt's Reflection:

I really don't remember much about this second stint
in the hospital, primarily because I was on a lot of
meds for my back pain. Remember that excruciating
pain? Well, it was relieved by two morphine pills a
day, Percocet from breakthrough pain, and then they
prescribed me a Valium at night to sleep. I was on so

many meds that I wasn't allowed to drive. At this point, I felt helpless.

Shay's Reflection:

We immediately knew that this journey wasn't about us from the first day. We just knew it by faith. Any opportunity we had to minister and share the love of Jesus, then we were going to do it. I would find myself thinking – God, is this the person who needs to feel your unconditional love? Is this the person who we are going through this journey for?? I never received a clear answer, but, we were committed to be purposeful and intentional in the journey.

 Shay Greenwood is with **Roosevelt Greenwood** and **4 others.**
September 15, 2016 · 🌐

···

Wednesday night youth service at Broadmoor is so fun! Your kids would love it. It's what captivated my children and one of the reasons we are at Broadmoor. It's not only fun, but it ministers. It personally ministered to me Wednesday. Noah was "rapping" during one of the songs. (Yes, rapping.) So I swung by church on my way back to the hospital. This picture is the epitome of the kind of love that Jesus has for us. Bryce is praying...she has the microphone. Notice the girl with her hands on the back of the people sitting next to her? That's **Anna Claire Holloway**. The boy sitting to her left is **Noah Javon Greenwood**...our son. A part of their prayer that night was for the Greenwood family. I was overwhelmed that these young people would think about our family. So sweet. Then, afterward **Kaitlyn Malouf** gave me a hug and then asked if she could pray for me. Young people. I love them! We can believe in them and not look down on their youthfulness. Witnessing their faith was so inspiring and gave me needed energy. Thank you!!

You all have overwhelmed us. God's love though should overwhelm us. Great lessons in this season for sure.

It feels like it has been a few months since the diagnosis. Literally. So much has happened. So much has been said. So much has been felt. So much has been done. And, even though it's been difficult...we are beyond grateful!! Grateful for a weight lifting injury, grateful for caring doctors and nurses, grateful for medical technology, grateful for friends who think for us, grateful for the sweet, encouraging messages, cards, food, money, sweet gifts of encouragement...every little thing means so much and is beyond amazing!!

And the prayers...people keep telling us that they haven't prayed so much in all their lives. So be it, right? God has us exactly where He wants us and it is good! And it's going to be good. We have that expectation. Roosevelt Greenwood is feeling good. He's emotional when he talks about his wife (me!) and the children. Of course! This is a really big deal and we are still trying to process it all. I still have this out of body experience when I talk about it...thinking...am I talking about my life?

We spent the last 4 days in the hospital. He was readmitted into the hospital on Monday for fever. He had a bacterial infection...that they fought with antibiotics. So, he's good now. We are being open about this fight because if one person's life is changed then we haven't wasted this challenge. We have allowed it to be used to help someone else. ...Even if it's just one. You really can't fight effectively in the dark. Are you hiding your challenge? Are you keeping it in the dark? We are stronger together I promise. I think I said that before. But it's true. I will probably say it again. To God be the glory for the things He has done!!

#greenwoodstrong
#rooseveltgreenwood

👍 Like   💬 Comment   ↪ Share

👍❤️ Michelle Mimi Davis and 196 others

10 shares

Roosevelt's Reflection:

I am so thankful for normalcy in our lives. Just because someone is sick, life does not stop - it's just a new normal. I am glad that Noah was able to participate in church activities that kept him engaged as well as football for both boys, ballet for Bria, and college for the Chandler.

Shay's Reflection:

Not only did I find myself feeling overwhelmed with caring for Roosevelt, I was overwhelmed with the thought of taking care of the kids and making sure that they were okay, too. We homeschool Adam, who happened to be 5 years old at the time, and he needed me. While we were in the hospital, he stayed with Chandler, who took off from school, or our friend Suzanne had him, or Bria's friend Stephanie kept him. I had to not focus on that fact so much and allow God to help me be okay with not being there for my children knowing that they were in good hands. The rest of the kids are all so independent. I knew that they were connecting with their friends and that they would reach out if they needed me. I made it a point to still attend what was important to them whenever I could. This day, I had to go home and get some things at home and swing by church to attend the youth service. It was just the encouragement that I needed.

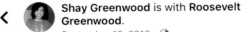

Shay Greenwood is with **Roosevelt Greenwood**.

September 19, 2016 · 🌐

12th day of the chemo pill.
4th day of radiation.
Only 13 days from diagnosis.
And, the Lord still sits on the throne of our lives! He says He will never leave us and we believe that!

On this day, we are so thankful that God orchestrated the radiation appointments for in the morning. After running a few errands. I had to pull over on the highway because **Roosevelt Greenwood** got sick. When we got home, he took a nap and ate and then felt good enough to attend Jacob's football game tonight. So thankful for a morning appointment. We feel like being able to go to the football game defeated any discouragement we may have felt. We will just keep pressing on, doing the next thing!

Continue to pray that God would keep the side effects at a minimal! Pray that the treatment is doing what it should do, and that those bad cells would start operating peacefully, in Jesus name! We have an appointment with the oncologist on Thursday.

We know that God has this all in His hands! We trust Him, because He's always faithful! Thank you so much for those of you who have already done so much. It helps us to feel strong going through this knowing that we have an army fighting with us! We love you all so much! 😇🖤
#greenwoodstrong #rooseveltgreenwood

Bria Greenwood
Chandler Greenwood
Noah Javon Greenwood
Jacob Greenwood

#greenwoodstrong

Roosevelt's Reflection:

As I think back to that day, I wondered then what kind of damage the rays were doing to my body. I would bring a wooden cross that was given to me by one of Bria's sweet friends. She told me to hold on to it while having my radiation treatment. I started praying, "Lord will you allow the radiation to kill all the bad cells and please preserve the good cells, in Jesus name Amen. The time went by so fast. Fifteen to 20 minutes, and I was outta there. The doctor said that I could get sick, and as I got sick on the way home, I thought...is this how it's going to be? Shay was ready to pull over. It ended up being the only time I ever threw up from my radiation or my chemo treatment. I am still so grateful for that fact.

Shay's Reflection:

Tears come to my eyes as I think about all that we had already been through in this short period of time. Twelve days from diagnosis. I would have never thought that we would be at this point dealing with cancer. I can tell that our eyes were tired. I remember walking into the Germantown High School Stadium with gratefulness. It was such a beautiful night for a game. After dealing with so much, we got to be outside and enjoy it. I was so grateful that Roosevelt could walk from the parking lot to the stadium seats. I was already recognizing the miracle of medicine. Yes, he was on a lot of it and couldn't drive while on it, but, I was grateful that we weren't still in the hospital. Anywhere but there was good right now.

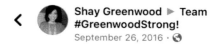
We are staying on the LEFT side of this picture! How about you?

No new news from the doctor.
Our urologist's name is Dr. Felix Gordon.
He took his time and was super patient.
I kept thinking he has a ton of patients and he is acting like we are the only one. We talked about the Germantown football game and then he sat down and settled in to ask Roosevelt about how he was feeling.

Roosevelt then asked a ton of questions...how does this happen, where did it come from? Etc. In a nutshell, it just happens...it confirmed Roosevelt's constant comment to me..."cancer is no respect of persons". African American men are more susceptible (only men have a prostate if you didn't know that already 😋), cancer in your family causes you to be more susceptible...nothing can really be done to prevent it. It is rare to get it so young and our boys should start being checked at age 35 for preventive reasons...studies show its genetic. It's also rare that it's so advanced in someone **Roosevelt Greenwood**'s age. He has a Gleason 9 rating which helps doctors to know how aggressive it is. It's rating goes from a 1-10. So, this is nothing new...his cancer is aggressive. Dr. Gordon encouraged Roosevelt to do what he is suppose to do...take the treatments, exercise, eat right, have faith, keep his mind focused on the possibilities. He said ultimately faith is what makes the difference. He wants to see him in 3 months and

wants us to see a medical oncologist just to make sure there isn't any other chemo treatments that we should consider.

So until then...we will continue to praise the Lord for His provision through our new life. He is faithful and we can trust Him. Thank you for praying! It makes a difference.

Wait for the Lord;
Be strong and let your heart take courage;
Yes, wait for the Lord. Psalms 27:14

#greenwoodstrong

God
Stills you
Reassures you
Leads you
Enlightens you
Forgives you
Calms you
Encourages you
Comforts you

Satan
Rushes you
Frightens you
Pushes you
Confuses you
Condemns you
Stresses you
Discourages you
Worries you

©GodFruits.com

👍 Like   💬 Comment   ↪ Share

👍💬 Sebrena Catchings Tillman and 95 others

Roosevelt's Reflection:

Dr. Gordon was cool; he was very thoughtful and insightful. He gave me hope. He told me of all the men in his family who had battled this disease, and he even told me that he would definitely one day have it because of the research that says he is so susceptible. Now, I must admit, I wasn't expecting to hear him say those words, but in a strange way, it brought me peace. He told me that I had too much testosterone. I didn't know a man could have too much testosterone. I always thought more was better, but not in this case.

Shay's Reflection:

I saw this list of how God operates and how satan operates. The way that satan operates was so familiar to me. It was exactly how I felt many days and nights as we were processing everything. I immediately knew I needed to print it out for encouragement. I found my thoughts would wonder into all the different scenarios we could face. It was exhausting. I was having to encourage not only myself but Roosevelt also. His mind was playing the same tricks on him. Playing what if games was not fun. Its debilitating and causes feelings of hopelessness.

Shay Greenwood was live.
September 28, 2016 · 🌐

Prostate cancer awareness month is now. Roosevelt says go get checked men!

We will reflect on God's goodness regardless of our circumstances! **Roosevelt Greenwood #greenwoodstrong**

8.7K Views

👍 Like   💬 Comment   ↪ Share

👍❤️😆 Michelle Mimi Davis and 548 others

49 shares

Roosevelt's Reflection:

This was 21 days out from my cancer diagnosis. God was already providing small miracles to help keep us encouraged, and we wanted to tell everyone about it. Life was changing for us in big ways. There were constant doctor's appointments. I already had a few hospital stays. I had side effects from the medicine I was taking. The hormone shots were giving me hot flashes. It was hard, but I felt encouraged and strong. It was good for me to share openly about what was going on.

In the video, we talked about a specific miracle. Cliff, a pastor at Broadmoor Baptist Church came, by the hospital during my initial stay and asked what he could specifically pray. Shay told him that I was having hiccups from the Casodex (chemo pill) I was taking. It was irritating more than anything. It would last 30-40 minutes after I would take it. Cliff prayed for it to leave, and I NEVER had another hiccup after that.

During that same time, Preston, another pastor from Broadmoor, asked if he could specifically pray for my back. He asked if he could lay his hands directly on my back and pray for healing. Of course, I didn't turn him down. I know the power of prayer, and I believe what the Bible says in James 5:14. Currently, I don't take any pain medicine for my back. It's a complete miracle that I'm not paralyzed from lesions that they found on my spine. Men are paralyzed from this disease, and I'm so thankful that I'm not one of them.

I'm determined to celebrate the small battles until we win the war.

Shay's Reflection:

I didn't realize how therapeutic it would be to share with our Facebook friends and family what was going on this us. Even though living day to day was difficult. We had tons of decisions to make about insurance, treatments, and all the overwhelming thoughts that happen with this kind of life crisis. I felt so much joy, though, knowing that a post or a video that we would share would bless someone and in turn bless us. I would watch Roosevelt get so much encouragement reading through all the comments. It was the best therapy for him. I was so grateful that the Lord led us to share openly. It was just what he needed.

We would try to text the friends and family who were not on Facebook and keep them posted. But, it was SO hard to think of whom we needed to keep posted. Social media was the best way for us to keep everyone informed. I felt badly when I would hear that someone felt out of the loop. It's amazing the amount of information you are being faced with on top of an already busy life. I knew that I had to let go of the responsibility of keeping everyone happy and know that my goal was Roosevelt and my family. We had to keep our head above water so we didn't feel like we were drowning. Facebook was definitely going to be the best mode of communication for me.

Shay Greenwood
October 5, 2016 · 🌐

We waste our cancer if we think that "beating" cancer means staying alive rather than cherishing Christ. Satan's and God's designs in our cancer are not the same. Satan designs to destroy our love for Christ. God designs to deepen our love for Christ. Cancer does not win if we die. It wins if we fail to cherish Christ. God's design is to wean us off the breast of the world and feast us on the sufficiency of Christ. It is meant to help us say and feel, "I count everything as loss because of the surpassing worth of knowing Christ Jesus my Lord" (Philippians 3:8) and to know that therefore, "to live is Christ, and to die is gain" (Philippians 1:21).

Thanks **Ronnie Humphrey** for your encouragement and passing on this booklet! We don't plan on wasting this opportunity.

Roosevelt Greenwood
Bria Greenwood
Chandler Greenwood
Jacob Greenwood
Noah Javon Greenwood
#greenwoodstrong

Read more here: Don't Waste Cancer by John Piper...

DOCUMENT.DESIRINGGOD.ORG
document.desiringgod.org
http://document.desiringgod.org/don-t-waste-your-cancer...

👍 Like　　💬 Comment　　↪ Share

👍💙 Michelle Mimi Davis and 111 others

9 shares

Roosevelt's Reflection:

When Shay suggested the book, *Don't Waste Cancer,* I felt very overwhelmed. I don't want the cancer in the first place. I know that things happen to you for the benefit of others. But, right now, I would like the cancer to go away. Metaphorically, cancer can be a number of things: loss of a job, a sick child, being homeless, divorce, death. You have to be able to find significance in how your journey can help someone else, and that's what this book reveals. When Shay read it to me in the hospital, I knew it was how we needed to see our situation, no matter how we were feeling.

Shay's Reflection:

I remember receiving a voicemail message on my phone from a man named Ronnie Humphrey. Roosevelt and I did a Facebook live video on Sept 12th, and I received a phone call that same day. I called Ronnie back and some how he saw the video from a friend of a friend sharing it and wanted to reach out to us to encourage us in this journey. This connection will forever be etched in my mind because Ronnie was a complete stranger. But, he wanted to share with us his testimony through prostate cancer and wanted us to know that we were not alone and that he would be praying for Roosevelt and me. He told us about the Don't Waste Cancer booklet by John Piper. I read the PDF online that day and then read it to Roosevelt. There were 10 powerful statements. When you read it, just replace the word cancer with the tough situation that you are going through right now. It applies to all the "cancers" of life. Such an encouraging perspective that life is NOT about us, but it's about God's work through us.

1 Peter 5:9 says, But resist him, firm in your faith, knowing that the same experiences of suffering are being accomplished by your brethren who are in the world. What an encouragement to know that there were others on the same journey. It was more encouragement that we needed to keep moving forward by faith.

We are Facebook friends with Ronnie and his wife, Janice. They represent the power of social media being used to connect people to have community, for encouragement, and ultimately to bring glory to God. Thank you, virtual BFF friends! We appreciate you more than you know!

Follow us here also: **https://www.facebook.com/groups/
1845299685690874/**

Update:
You know how when you are at a loss for words? I
sometimes can get that way even though **Roosevelt
Greenwood** says that I don't ever need to prepare for a
speech because I can filibuster for at least 30 minutes
without stopping. 😀 How-ev-er, experiencing my husband
having cancer and all the information from doctors that
comes with it, gives me a lack of words because it's almost
too much to take...too much for a person to handle.

We met with the medical oncologist, Dr. Qu, for the first time
last week. He was perplexed as to how Roosevelt could be
his age (48 years old tomorrow!) and have Stage 4
metastatic cancer...he confirmed that Roosevelt has
prostate cancer that has spread to his bones...his back,
hips, femur...and to his lymph nodes and there is also a few
small spots on his lung. It's really still unbelievable.

(Have you seen my handsome husband? He looks good,
sounds good, feels good. He is himself...playing the organ at
church every single Sunday since being diagnosed Sept.
7th...attending the kids activities like normal, joking and
laughing like normal...except for his naps after the Monday-
Friday radiation.)

It's hard to hear all of this going on in his body...when what
we see when we look at him, does not look like what is

unseen.

Dr. Qu gave us a new plan of attack...a new battle plan. It
includes Roosevelt having out-patient surgery in the
morning to install a port...he will finish his radiation on his
bones this week on Wednesday. He will then start chemo
treatments on the 25th. He has been taking a hormone
based chemo pill...but it's the infusion that he is about to
take and the radiation to his prostate later that will help to
prolong his life. It is difficult to write that. Prolong his life?!
What in the world does that mean? It means that just like
getting a diagnosis of Diabetes or M.S...my sweet husband

47

will be treated with this cancer for the rest of his life. ...We have had to let that sink in.

It means there is no cure...it's a chronic illness, and (thank you, Jesus) it's "highly treatable". I have let those two words sink in. And what we also know is regardless of the unseen...God can heal him!! I wish you could hear Roosevelt talk about the story of Daniel and the 3 Hebrew boys...they were captured and told to bow down to a false god or else they would be killed...but they were not going to bow down because they knew and believed that if God didn't deliver them, that He could. And that's what we are sure about...if God doesn't heal Roosevelt physically, we believe that He can heal!! And, we can pray for that healing and ask Him to get the glory out of this situation regardless!! Just like a little child who asks over and over and over again for what they want, we can ask our Heavenly Father for what we desire, all for His glory and honor. God created us for HIS pleasure...for HIS glory. And that's what we hope for and desire through all of this. We believe God. We trust God. We love Him and know without a shadow of a doubt that He loves us. And we feel it. We know that He is present with

us...orchestrating every single step of the way.

2 Corinthians 4:8-12..."We are hard pressed on every side, but not crushed; perplexed, but not in despair; persecuted, but not abandoned; struck down, but not destroyed. We always carry around in our body the death of Jesus, so that the life of Jesus may also be revealed in our body. For we who are alive are always being given over to death for Jesus' sake, so that his life may also be revealed in our mortal body. So then, death is at work in us, but life is at work in you."

Roosevelt's high school classmate gave him a "battle" name..."Rooseveltus". He is a warrior and knows that he's not fighting alone. Are you fighting with us? It encourages us to know that we are in this together.

Please pray for all that I just detailed...Pray for continued wisdom of the medical team. Pray for peace for our family...that the Lord would continue to comfort us and bring us to Him continually for that peace and comfort. As well, that He alone would get the glory from our lives no matter what we are going through.

If you don't know the love of Jesus...if you follow us, our prayer is that you get to know who He is personally. He loves you more than you can even handle. Truly, we are seeing that through this. Thank you to all of our friends and family that have literally been the hands and feet of Jesus in our lives. If you have done anything in regards to our family. You know who you are. The love is overwhelming. Thank you isn't enough. It definitely makes me at a loss for words even though my husband never thinks that's possible. We love

you all!!

#greenwoodstrong
#rooseveltgreenwood
Bria Greenwood
Chandler Greenwood
Noah Javon Greenwood
Jacob Greenwood

Roosevelt's Reflection:

During this time, I always had the thought of what's next. After 25 rounds of radiation to my hip and spine, it's now time to take chemotherapy. From all that I read, this would be poison that they are putting in my body that's designed to kill the bad cancer cells, but it can kill good cells as well. This is scary. How will my body react to the chemotherapy? Will I be sick? Will I have energy? How will it transform my body? These are all the questions I have in the back of my mind. I have often said that I'm not afraid to die because of my faith. But, I must admit this process was scary to me. Right now, I feel good even though I just went through radiation. This is when I have to really rely upon God and trust that everything is going to be okay. Shay and I made a decision that we would trust what Dr. Qu told us. He has a great reputation for being smart. I determined that I would trust that the Lord would give him the wisdom to know how to treat my body for the best possible chance to be healed.

Shay's Reflection:

It stabs me in the heart when I think about Roosevelt having an INCURABLE disease like Stage 4 metastatic prostate cancer. It punches me in the gut. I feel an emptiness in my heart like you wouldn't believe. Everything in our life has changed so much. We live a new normal life. And, yet, we are still the same. I remember being strong at this appointment, knowing that God would give me enough strength to hear what I needed to hear and follow the doctor's orders. I knew that chemo would be the next step. I was part of every prostate cancer support group on Facebook. Prostate cancer seems to be a very unique cancer because it directly impacts a man masculinity. This was also very difficult for us to hear. This journey was hard, and it would get harder.

Bria Greenwood is with **Roosevelt Greenwood**.

October 17, 2016 · 🌐

Happy birthday to my Daddy!! 🙂 He is the epitome of a man that walks by faith, and not by sight (2 Cor. 5:7)! It has been so evident in the way he is walking through his diagnosis of stage four, metastatic prostate cancer. His cancer has now spread to his bones, back, hips, femur, lymph nodes, and there are some little spots on his lung. And, even with all of that, his faith in the Lord is not shaken! Because He knows that the God we serve is never changing, faithful, always listening, and is Jehovah Rapha, our Healer!

I'm amazed, and challenged by him everyday! He is SO strong, and has confidence in our Father, and trusts Him completely. This morning he will have a port installed, and will begin chemo on the 25th. Please continue to pray that the Lord would perform a miracle! Thank you everyone who has been praying and interceding for us. We love you so much!
"Those who know Your name trust in You, for You, Lord, have never forsaken those who seek You." (Psalm 9:10)

 Love   Comment   Share

 You, Michelle Mimi Davis and 367 others

2 shares

Bria's Reflection:

Bria's perspective (1st born daughter, age 20 at Roosevelt's diagnosis):

Sometimes life seems unbearable. Sometimes it makes a 180 degree turn. Wednesday, September 7, 2016 was that moment for me. Mom called me from the hospital and said, "Hey, where are you guys? You need to get the boys and come to the hospital."

I asked several times, "Why?", but she wouldn't tell me.

I didn't really know what to think. All Dad had gone to the hospital for was to get an MRI for nerve pain in his leg, so we thought that maybe a family member was there to surprise us or something.

When we walked into the hospital room, we saw Chandler crying across the room. That's when I felt my heart and stomach drop. I knew then that something was really wrong.

Mom, with tears in her eyes, told us that dad was diagnosed with stage four metastatic prostate cancer.

Normal PSA numbers for your prostate should be 4...Dad's was 1490!

The cancer had spread to other parts of his body, and the doctor said it was too late to do surgery because the cancer wasn't contained.

I feel like I'm in an out of body experience as I'm writing this...is this really happening to my family?

People say, "God won't put more on you than you can bear." That's not true at all!

He most definitely does because it causes you to have to rely on Him for everything we need.

Your trials may seem unbearable, until you take your thoughts captive, and remember that your relationship with an all-powerful God makes it bearable!

Cancer is not a death sentence, but it sure does sting. But, I find my rest, security, and hope in the Lord.

After we went home that Wednesday, I didn't get any sleep. The next day I got a message from a friend from church, and she said she was bringing over groceries and a freezer full of food!

I didn't allow myself to let all of my emotions out at the hospital because I felt that I had to be strong for my siblings. So, when I was awake by myself the next morning listening to worship music, I broke down.

As I was crying, my best friend Stephanie knocked on the door. She came in and comforted me for a while.

She came to watch Adam while I went to Ballet Mag.

After devotions that morning at Ballet Mag, everyone gathered around me and prayed for Dad and our family.

I don't think I've ever cried so much in my life. I couldn't even describe the feeling. You always see this stuff happen to other people, and you sympathize with them, but you truly don't understand how they feel, until it happens to you or your family.

I've been doing a devotional from the First 5 app on brokenness.

Brokenness reveals the beauty of Christ inside of us and others as they're praying for us.

Jesus is the only answer to life's troubles. It's not IF we have troubles, it's WHEN we have them.

It's guaranteed that Christ will be magnified, if we allow Him to work through our brokenness.

The almighty, all-powerful God is the One who will see us through. He comforts. He saves. He is near. He delivers. He gives peace. He gives joy.

He answers when I call on His name, because He's a faithful God that's never changing.

He provides stability, and we can rely on Him. This is what we're going to do. We're going to stand unshakable, but shapeable in this trial, because we stand on the Rock that's immovable.

I'm still processing everything. We definitely feel attacked from the enemy. He wants to destroy our family because he knows what we stand for and Whom we serve. He doesn't like it, and he permanently wants to steal our joy. But, mourning may endure for a night, but JOY comes in the morning (Ps. 30:5).

In the moments where I'm battling my thoughts, the Holy Spirit reminds me of the Scriptures that I've hidden in my heart.

Doctors say that Dad's cancer is treatable, but not curable. But, God says it's healable!

My God is the God of the impossible. Nothing is too hard for Him.

I don't understand how people who don't know the Lord get through something like this...they have no hope.

But, we have this hope as an anchor for our soul.

I know that He sees us, and isn't taken by surprise. He has prepared us by rooting and grounding us in His Word and with a solid understanding of His character.

We've gone through a F5 tornado, two miscarriages, loss of Dad's job, loss of our dream home, losing Grandad and Grandmom to cancer, and now this...

He brought us through all of those trials, and He'll be faithful to bring us through this one.

He's the same God yesterday, today, and forever. He's still good even in this devastating time.

Shay Greenwood
November 6, 2016 · 🌐

Praise God that we don't look like what we are going through! God works in our suffering and we can trust Him! **Roosevelt Greenwood #greenwoodstrong**

👍 Like   💬 Comment   ↪ Share

😮😲😋 Michelle Mimi Davis and 692 others

2 shares

Roosevelt's Reflection:

During the first treatment, all I could think about was what people say about chemotherapy being poison and that it attacks the cancer cells as well as the good cells. I also thought about how it would affect me physically, and I wondered if I would be too sick to function. I was a mess. Many times I rationalized not doing the treatment. I was already at stage 4. Maybe I should decline the chemotherapy and live the best life I can live until I'm called home to live with Jesus. Then, after thinking all of those negative thoughts, my spirit would say, "I will live and not die," and that's what I had to hold onto.

Shay's Reflection:

This picture was taken at our friends' Brad & Chelsey's wedding. We knew the first chemo treatment would be a few days before their wedding, and our plans were to play it by ear. They were getting married in Natchez, MS which is just a few hours from where we lived. We planned on driving there and coming back on the same day. The first chemo treatment was a daunting time because we didn't know what to expect. The first day of his treatment, he felt a little queasy and took a Zofran. But, other than that, it didn't seem to be too bad. I think it was more emotionally exhausting for the both of us knowing that he was injected with poison. It's almost too much to even think about. We were the only ones in the room the first time we had chemo, which was great. I remember packing my bag with my calendar—because I was still running a business—and I brought a book and my bible study and honestly, I don't think I did anything but mindless scroll through Facebook and chat about nothing.

After the first couple of times receiving chemo, we knew that the first few days weren't too bad, but then days 4-10 were the hardest with bone pain and fatigue. He even had a time that he contracted Strep throat because his white blood cell counts were low, so he had to go back in the hospital to be treated and watched. When you have fever at this stage, it's never a good thing. I remember being SO tired in this picture. I was mostly weary from our diagnosis and all that comes with it as a wife, mom, and now caregiver. This was the first picture that I remember taking saying that we didn't seem to look like what we were going through. We were truly walking by faith.

Chandler Greenwood is with **Roosevelt Greenwood** and **2 others.**
November 12, 2016 ·

Noah shaved his head for Dad 🖤 #likefatherlikeson #GreenwoodStrong

Make Profile Picture

Love   Comment   Share

You, Michelle Mimi Davis and 1K others

13 shares

Noah's Reflection: (son to Roosevelt & Shay, 16 years old at the time of diagnosis):

It's crazy when you watch movies and read articles about cancer; you never really think about it affecting your life. You basically think about it as if it is an anomaly that rarely happens to people. My life was pretty normal at the time. It was my junior season of football, and I was having a good year. When you talk about a dramatic shift in your life, it doesn't get any crazier than this.

It was a Wednesday, and I had just gotten out of football practice. I was ready to go to church that day and hangout with some friends. I knew my dad was at the hospital because he thought he injured his back during a workout. I didn't think anything of it, and I'm sure nobody else in my family did either. I was in the midst of making a peanut butter and jelly sandwich when all of a sudden my oldest sister, Bria, got off of the phone with my mother and proceeded to tell us we needed to go to the hospital. We were both questioning it. My brother even jokingly stated "What if he has cancer?" See? It's like cancer is so rare, nobody ever thinks about it. Little did we know. We made our way to the hospital, thinking nothing of the trip. To be honest, I thought that they were surprising us, like my grandmother or aunt was in town, or maybe he had to be in a wheelchair for a few weeks. Nothing too extreme. Once we opened those doors to the room, all I remember seeing was my sister, Chandler, sitting across the room crying (which wasn't new to me because she can be emotional at times). It did startle me a little bit, and I looked into my mother's eyes. All I saw was a woman that was trying to be strong for her children but was breaking on the inside. Only other time I had seen her like that was when she told us our grandfather had died. She uttered the words, "Your father has cancer." At first I was taken aback by the words. Like cancer? Nah MY father doesn't have cancer. What even is cancer? I've only really heard of it in magazines and on TV. All I knew about cancer was that it kills a lot of people. I let out all the crying that day. I remember calling one of my friends and telling her, "We think my dad has cancer." My sister overheard me and shook her head saying, "No, he DOES have cancer." That's when it hit me, and I just sat on the floor crying. To be honest, I knew cancer was a killer, but after that day, I never actually thought my father was going to die. Weeks passed, and people would come up to me and say, "I'm sorry for what has happened." I would think, "Why are you saying sorry to me? I'm not the one with cancer." Also, I didn't want people to pity me because of what my father was going through. I was strong because my mother and father were so strong. I never thought my father's life was in danger because I knew that if he died, he was going to Heaven, and I'd see him again. But also, God gave me peace in knowing that he wasn't going to take him from me anytime soon. I would cry because I felt for my dad. He was pretty young. He had children he still had to raise, and he liked being active. I knew that cancer would restrict him from doing a lot of those things he loved and seeing him constantly feel bad, taking medicines, and resting was painful because I knew he didn't want to do any of that. I got through it because the Lord placed an awesome church family and friends around me. If it wasn't for the constant texts, calls, and invitations to hangout and talk, I wouldn't have gotten through it. That's why I feel relationships are essential in your life. God places people in your life to remind you of who you are and Whose you are. No matter what happened to my father, he won. He either got to spend eternity with Jesus, or he could still kick it with us down here for a little more longer. That reassurance is what kept me going.

Roosevelt's Reflection:

"Wow" is the adjective I would use for this memory. After about two or three treatments, the Chemo took out my hair. I imagine for men this is not that big of a deal, because we can just rock the bald look. I have a pretty nice shaped head, so no big deal. But, honestly, I must admit, I cried. I have actually cried more in the last 3 years than in any point in my life. I remember waking up in the early morning hours and pulling on my hair as it was coming out in patches. I was not crying because I had such beautiful Samson locks. Now as I reflect on it, it was the fear of the unknown that had me in such an emotional state. God is so good, because it seemed to me that every time I had a down moment, the Lord would send me a positive moment, and this was truly one of them. Noah, my oldest son, was 16 years old at the time, and he had grown out his hair, so I know it was a big deal for him to cut it all off to show support for me. It's the small things that count. I love my son for thinking about me and wanting to support me. All of my kids have done this for me, and I'm so thankful for them.

Shay's Reflection:

I remember vividly when Roosevelt's hair started falling out. As I laid in the bed, I could see him go into the bathroom and look at his hair. I encouraged him to shave it. To me, it was better to have some control over it. I thought he looked really handsome bald, but I knew it bothered him. At this point, we were praying that the chemo was doing it's job against the bad cells in his body.

Bo N Kim Magoun is with **Suzanne Hollingshead** and **Shay Greenwood.**
November 14, 2016 · 👥   ···

Help support the Greenwood family during this season of their life. Get a bracelet to support the family and remember to pray for them daily. $2 let me know how many you want!!
#greenwoodstrong

Roosevelt's Reflection:

When you are going through difficulties, it takes a village or army to help you fight, and the support shown from our family and friends did just that. It is a bit overwhelming to think about the love shown to me and my family. The last thing I wanted Shay to have to worry about was handling the financial responsibilities on her own. As a man, it is my responsibility to provide for my family, and at this point, with the amount of gas going back and forth to appointments, hospital stays, doctor's appointment, and the expenses were starting to add up. Having Kim set up a fundraiser for us gave me a glimpse into understanding that ultimately God is our provider.

Shay's Reflection:

Our friend, Kim Magoun, asked if she could help us financially by offering these #Greenwoodstrong bracelets for $2. It makes me emotional just typing that. There is a heavy financial burden that is placed on individuals and their families with a cancer diagnosis. It's beyond our thinking if you haven't ever experienced it. You need more money for everything, and what a blessing this extra cash provided for us at the time that we needed it most! We were overwhelmed with the love of God through this. It

63

overwhelms us still until this day. We are forever grateful, and it has taught us to pay it forward and never hesitate in giving and supporting those who are in need. Because we have experienced this, instead of asking people, "What do you need?", we now know exactly what they need and we are more than willing to give it.

Shay Greenwood
November 28, 2016 · 🌐

"Anti-cancer salad"
Recipe from www.chrisbeatcancer.com
Roosevelt Greenwood: It tastes like you picked everything fresh out of the ground. 😂

He said I made him too much. Poor baby.

"You are eating to live! Not living to eat!"
"Man has a responsibility
We are leaving the results to God."
"You are being rebuilt"
-Shay, all my sayings for the day.
#greenwoodstrong

👍 Like   💬 Comment   ➤ Share

👍❤️😋 Cathy Wilkes Helms and 171 others

4 shares

Roosevelt's reflections....

The new diet took some getting used to. My sweet wife wanted me to eat salad and drink water, and I just couldn't get there. Thankfully, I had a good appetite and the chemo didn't destroy my taste buds. I must say that now, through a pretty lengthy process I have cut a lot of sugar out of my diet. I believe that all our days are numbered, but I also believe that God can change his mind and give you more days. If I can show him that I'm trying, maybe he will say yes to many more years with my wife and children.

Shay's Reflection:

It's the most amazing thing to me the amount of messages that FLOODED my Facebook inbox about the different diets Roosevelt should implement, or the different treatments that he should receive RATHER than what we were doing already. We know without a shadow of a doubt that these people cared about us, and we are thankful for that care. Honestly, it overwhelmed me, and I created a message on my notepad that was a standard message for messages like this. It stated something like, "we are following and trusting our doctor right now, but thanks so much for your information, etc. I can't remember who suggested that to us, but it was a great way to release the burden of thinking through every single suggestion. It can definitely make you weary and it made me weary. Again, I was grateful for the concern, just weary from our situation.

We found a website called Chris Beats Cancer. It had great information from a guy named Chris who used a strict plant-based diet to help cure his cancer. Although he had surgery to remove his cancer, and they were able to take it all out, instead of him having radiation and chemotherapy as his doctors suggested, he opted to change his diet. Cancer cells feed off of sugar, and diet can play a huge role in helping your body heal itself in the process.

One of the things that I would tell Roosevelt repeatedly, especially on those radiation and chemo days where he didn't want to eat anything healthy was that God decides the number of days we have." We aren't going to hold onto anything too tightly. There are healthy, athletic people who die everyday from cancer or heart attacks. We will do what we are supposed to do and pray that God blesses it over and beyond what we could imagine or think.

Roosevelt made many changes to his diet. He has eliminated sugar and eats mostly poultry, fish, and vegetables. He drinks PH balanced water. You can purchase a Pitcher of Life Alkaline Water pitcher from Amazon. Cancer can't live in a high alkaline body or so they say. You can also purchase Essentia Water as well.

Matt Mayo is with **Suzanne Hollingshead** and **4 others.**   •••
December 1, 2016 · Shared via AddThis · ⊕

Show your support for **#greenwoodstrong** by purchasing one of these AWESOME tshirts! All profits go to the #greenwoodstrong family.Help us reach our goal of 500 shirts sold by the end of December 2016!
Shay and Roosevelt Greenwood are the loving parents of five children between the ages of 4 and 20. Roosevelt was recently diagnosed with metastatic prostate cancer and is currently receiving treatment. The Greenwoods have overcome many obstacles before and have faith that they will overcome this hard situation. His family and friends are praying for complete healing. #GreenwoodStrong

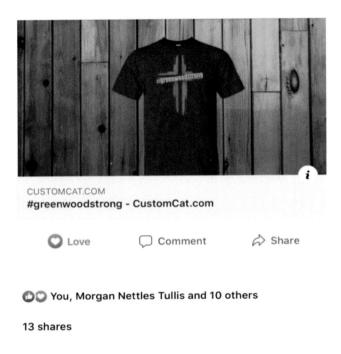

Love   Comment   Share

You, Morgan Nettles Tullis and 10 others

13 shares

Shay's Reflection:

This is one of the other posts about these t-shirts which captured my thoughts:

What amazing friends and family we have! Seriously. What you all do for us is more than we can handle. It makes me so teary as I write this.

During this journey, we have found, and I've said this before, that words aren't enough anymore. They seem minuscule in comparison to how we feel.

As traumatic as our situation is, God's love from His people overwhelms it. He constantly reminds us we aren't alone—that He is with us. We are so grateful.

Thank you, Matt, for designing these t-shirts as a gift to us. (Click the link below if you want to purchase one.) Thank you Terri for encouraging, praying, and supporting us by doing this. We love you! And I can't wait to sport my t-shirt!! To me, it means we are defeating the enemy. He can't win! We won't let him. We win regardless. And we will continue to be strong and courageous! (Joshua 1:9)

As you wear your t-shirt, I know you will pray for Roosevelt and our family. And we will pray for you as well!! We love each one of you!!

One of the most powerful things that God led us to do was to share Roosevelt's diagnosis through Facebook. This wasn't just our story to share, but it was God's story. So, when God led others to suggest how they wanted to help, we let them. What an amazing gift it was to see how the Lord was going to provide for us. A cancer diagnosis will break your finances. I know now that people who are going through something like this can't fight this battle and be worried about money at the same time. Others knew more than we knew. And, we are so grateful for so many people who allowed God to use them. We had countless people provide money to pay for groceries, cell phone bills, rent, snacks in the hospital, school lunches, and the list goes on and on. If you are one of those people, we can't thank you enough.

Roosevelt's Reflection:

For those of you who know me, these acts of kindness are too hard to comprehend. I learn daily that you allow people to help you because if you don't, you cut off their blessing from God. I don't want to cut anyone off from being blessed by God. It's a humbling experience to be on the receiving end of someone's gift. My dad taught me that when someone does something for you, receive it and say thank you. So, I'm saying thank you. You all know who you are.

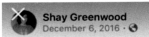

Shay Greenwood
December 6, 2016 ·

When you go to a follow up radiology appointment and they say:

✓ You are doing great!

✓ You look great!

✓ I'm a positive Doctor, but I would tell you if you weren't doing great. I'm not just talking.

✓ This treatment doesn't have to work, but it is.

✓ This doesn't have to go this way, it could be worse.

✓ Your nurse starts crying tears of joy after explaining how she was so heartbroken for us the first time we came in and she is so thankful to God for how Roosevelt is doing.

✓ A PSA level doesn't go from a 9.4 to .2 in one month normally. It normally lowers in small increments if at all.

Tears.
This is another win for **#greenwoodstrong**.
Roosevelt Greenwood says we will celebrate each little battle until we win this war.
We couldn't do it without you.
We don't want to.
We want to be together when it's hard.
And we want to celebrate with you when it's good.
We are on the battlefield for the long haul and we know you are fighting with us.
Thank you for praying!
Bless you!
We love you a lot.
We take nothing for granted.
We praise God from where all blessings flow!

So many of you ask how you can be helpful...keep praying is our prayer! Our friends have gone above and beyond to do these things for us and I get admonished when I don't post the links of how else you can help. (Which is difficult for us.) But here they are...

http://www.customcat.com/campaign/greenwoodstrong

https://www.youcaring.com/roosevelt-

We want to be together when it's hard.
And we want to celebrate with you when it's good.
We are on the battlefield for the long haul and we know you
are fighting with us.
Thank you for praying!
Bless you!
We love you a lot.
We take nothing for granted.
We praise God from where all blessings flow!

So many of you ask how you can be helpful...keep praying is
our prayer! Our friends have gone above and beyond to do
these things for us and I get admonished when I don't post
the links of how else you can help. (Which is difficult for us.)
But here they are...

http://www.customcat.com/campaign/greenwoodstrong

https://www.youcaring.com/roosevelt-
greenwood-648335
#greenwoodstrong
Bria Greenwood
Chandler Greenwood
Noah Javon Greenwood
Jacob Greenwood

 Eric Richards and 1.1K others   358 Comments

Roosevelt's Reflection:

I had been taught, as a child, that healing is directly related to your belief that you would be healed. Once I received the Stage 4 diagnosis, even though I would brace myself for bad news at each visit, I always believed that I would be healed. It was this belief that always made me feel like a winner.

Shay's Reflection:

This post says it all. We are so grateful for the progress. Truly, we were praising the Lord for the hope of this appointment. Jennifer was the nurse for Dr. Johnson. I think I knew the severity of Roosevelt's diagnosis. But, I had armor on daily for the things we were facing. To hear Jennifer actually cry saying that she was so sad over hearing his initial diagnosis and seeing the pain that he was in, but she was so grateful that the treatments were working. She cried because of the happiness of his progress and healing through the treatments. What I heard was, "He was so bad off, I didn't think he had any hope." Whew!! Thank you Jesus for the healing!!

LaJesca Woodard was live.
December 11, 2016 · 👥

•••

Roosevelt Greenwood and **Shay Greenwood**
This family is one of the best that I know!!!! I am so glad that I've had the opportunity to get to know them. Even during their trials, they are still encouraging and uplifting others. God bless you all #greenwoodstrong

3.3K Views

👍 Like   💬 Comment   ↗ Share

😊👍 **Roosevelt Greenwood and 215 others**

49 shares

Roosevelt's Reflection:

For those of you who don't know, I am a musician. I play the organ, and I have been serving in the music department for thirty-four years in various churches. One of those churches is Mary Grove Missionary Baptist Church in Sharon, MS. They loved on us through hosting a benefit program. I joked with my wife and told her that it has been my experience with programs like this that they are held when you are on your way out. But I will be the exception! "I shall live and not die." That was going to be my ongoing motto for myself. Thank you to Mary Grove Missionary Baptist Church and other area churches for blessing us in such a loving, supportive way. It was another example of how the Lord was providing for us.

Shay's Reflection:

Please make sure that you check out the video! Roosevelt said thank you. He sang, our daughters sang, and we worshipped the One True God who hears our prayers. We praised and loved Jesus for what He had done and what we believed that He was going to do. What a blessing to do that with the precious members of Mary Grove MB Church and other churches who wanted to support Roosevelt in the time that he needed the encouragement the most.

I've learned so much during this time up until this moment. Moments like this have reminded me over and over again that "the generous man will be prosperous, and he who waters will himself be watered." Proverbs 11:25. I'm a natural encourager and to get encouragement in my time of need was amazing. The community of Canton, MS was where he grew up and where he gave back through being a church musician and an administrator for the Canton Public School District. It was a gift to see the amount of support from his family and friends through this event. The support is what kept him going during this time.

 Jacob Greenwood is at **Disney's Magic Kingdom.**
December 21, 2016 · Lake Buena Vista, FL · 👥 ···

Had fun at Disneyworld with the fam! 😊 💯 😎 **Shay Greenwood**
    Roosevelt Greenwood
    Chandler Greenwood
    Bria Greenwood
    Noah Javon Greenwood

❤️ Love   💬 Comment

👍❤️😮 You, Michelle Mimi Davis and 45 others

Jacob's perspective (4th child, son to Roosevelt & Shay, 14 years old at the time of diagnosis):

I vividly remember certain details of the day of my Dad's diagnosis. I remember coming home after a long day of school and going to sleep on the couch. My sister, Bria, woke me up and told me that we had to go to the hospital. I didn't know why we would need to go to the hospital if he was just getting his leg checked out. My brother, Noah, and my sister piled into the car and headed toward the hospital. On the way, we discussed possible scenarios that could have happened to dad. I don't remember every scenario, but I do remember stating, "it's not like he has cancer or anything." We all laughed it off as an impractical notion. We arrived at the hospital and made it up to my father's room. Before entering, my brother, sister, and I were laughing and being loud, but once we entered, it was like all of the joy we were feeling had been sucked away. I looked at my dad, who was lying in the bed with a vacant, glazed look on his face, and I remember looking at my sister, Chandler, who had arrived before us, with tears in her eyes. My mother told us to sit down. She paused for a minute and then stated, "your dad has cancer." She continued to talk, but I don't remember anything that she said. Everything sort of froze in time. I just sat there in my chair with my head down. No tears. Nothing but shock. Not long after she told us, my grandma Ozie walked in, and that joy that I said was sucked away came back in an instant. She came in with such joy that you couldn't help but feel a little better about the horrible situation.

I didn't cry until later that night. I was in the hallway of the hospital, and my pastor, Rob Futral, came up to me and gave me a hug. I don't know what it was, whether it was his embrace or the fact that I had held in my emotions up until this point, but tears suddenly started running down my face. I don't remember if he said anything to me or not, but I do remember that he did not let me go.

The rest of the night was a daze. I remember somehow getting home, and one of my friends reminded me that we had a quiz the next day. I studied and went to sleep.

My brother and I went to school the next day even though I didn't really want to. I sat in my first block class waiting to take my quiz when a kid came into class with a red note (red is never good) that said the counselors needed me in their office. I remember seeing my brother walking with someone crying, and in my mind I was like, "oh no", because I knew they wanted to talk about my Dad's diagnosis. They sat us down in a room, and I remember Mrs. Volk coming in and praying over my brother and me and quoting a scripture that I cannot remember. Then, Coach Shramek came in and talked to us. I don't remember all that he said, but what I do remember is that he gave us a pass to show our teachers in case we need to get away from everything and go to the field house to chill out.

Later that day my coach got me out of my 4th block class and had me come down to the field house. It was a Thursday because the Varsity team was having their usual meeting. I sat towards the back, and at the end of the meeting, Coach Shramek called my brother and me up to the front and broke the news to the team about my father. They crowded around us and prayed over us. During the prayer, I started to get tears in my eyes, but I held it in because I don't like people seeing me emotional.

A few days after that was a blur. So many overwhelming events and life changes occurred for my family that it was hard to keep up with, but our church, friends, and family helped ease the heavy load that was cast upon us.
Galatians 6:2 says, "bear one another's burdens, and so fulfill the law of Christ." And what a myriad of people did for my family is a perfect example of God's law being fulfilled.

Roosevelt's Reflection:

At this point, I was just thankful that I was winning the battle with Stage 4 cancer. My family, Bryan and Robbie, were gracious enough to extend their timeshare to our family, and we were off to Disney World: this was definitely another moment that made me pause and say, "thank you".

Shay's Reflection:

Everyone needs a vacation from their everyday lives. I firmly believe that. This was one of those times. When Bryan and Robbie offered us the timeshare, we said yes quickly because by this time we were tired and just needed a break from our regular routine and treatments. We planned for Roosevelt's chemo treatment to be done the following week when we returned. Until then, we were grateful for the break.

Our church life group – our Sunday school class - gave us money for Christmas, which came in handy for this trip and relieved such a huge financial burden. This was definitely another example of the overwhelming love of God through His people.

This trip was a hard trip for me. All I wanted to do was lay in the bed and do nothing. But, I also wanted my family to experience Disney World. Even though I was tired, we had a great time together for sure, and it was a trip that we will never forget.

C Spire
December 22, 2016 · 🌐

···

Watch Christmas Wish 2016— We hit the road and surprised three customers by making their wishes come true. http://cspi.re/uQbE307neoS

54.1K Views

♡ Love   💬 Comment   ↱ Share

👍❤️😊 You, Sylvia Newman-Green and 287 others

315 shares

Roosevelt's Reflection:

When Shay and the kids read the note from Cspire that we won a gift of $10,000, I was overwhelmed with emotions. I was emotional anyway because of the hormone shots I was on, but this was over the top for me. Then, I learned that our friends wrote into them about our situation and that was too much for me to handle as well. I cried. I was at a place where I felt helpless to help my family. I felt desperate. And, this felt like I was being rescued from my negative thoughts about my situation at least for a little while. I am forever grateful for the kindness of our friends that would go out of their way to bless us with this special gift of thoughtfulness. And, we are thankful to Cspire for choosing us. What a way to bless a family!

Shay's Reflection:

From my window, I saw my friends coming across my yard...Millie, Toni, Cathy, Chelsey, Suzanne...I remember feeling was so confused, but so happy to see my friends at the same time. There was a big RV parked outside our house and other people I didn't know coming up to my house, and everyone had on Santa hats. To our surprise, we were one of three Cspire customers chosen for a monetary gift of $10,000! We were shocked and beyond thankful for such a generous gift. During this time, we needed the money and it eliminated a financial stressor for us for sure. More than that though, we were in awe over the friends who wrote in about our situation and that we were chosen to be one of the winners. It brings tears to my eyes just writing this. We needed hope and encouragement especially during the holiday season. There are so many decisions that needed to be made that overwhelmed me especially. This was a tangible way that helped me to know that God saw our need and supplied it above and beyond what we knew possible. The money is long gone, but this still gives me so much hope for any circumstance or trial we face. God is always there and He cares. I needed to hold onto that.

Shay Greenwood
January 6, 2017 · 🌐

#greenwoodstrong Update: The last 4-5 days have been hard. Period.
...Physically for Roosevelt, mentally, and emotionally for us. Those are just the facts.
Being children of the King, we have had to straighten our crowns many times this week. Being reminded of what life is really all about. Coming face to face with the raw emotions that come with the reality of what we are dealing with. Cancer. It sucks. (We don't use that word, but there isn't another one better to describe it. 😔) ...And, then our hearts turn to God. And the reality of cancer is kicked in the face because we know our God who controls it all.
Who is by our side and promises to never leave.
Who holds the stars, sun, moon in the sky.
Who is faithful and true.
Who created us before the foundation of the world.
Who created us for His pleasure, His glory, His purposes.
Who says things like, "Have you considered my servant Roosevelt?"
Who gave up His only son Jesus to save us from our sins, but more importantly to prove His righteousness.
Who enables us to have (seriously) joy and peace through hard circumstances.
Who doesn't make sense sometimes, but we believe Him by faith
Who is a God who heals...and we will continue to believe for that continued healing for my sweet husband, in the name of Jesus. And, even if he doesn't provide that physical healing, we know that He can. And eternal life with Jesus is better than anything this world can provide. (Can you only

imagine when that day comes...when you are forever in His arms?) We know that to be true by faith. We can't help that. Until then we fight this earthly, spiritual fight with everything we have. No matter how exhausting. We continue to move forward. Doing the next thing that God has planned for us knowing that He is working out every detail. We don't dare give up now! ...And we will forever give Him praise!

Roosevelt Greenwood had his chemo treatment on the 29th and about day 3, it became hard and then harder and now feeling like he's turning a corner today (we are praying)! Thank you for your calls and texts...they mean more than you know. We try to laugh a lot during this time. (Thus, funny Facebook posts) It provides good times regardless of what the reality is. We welcome laughter and seek it. We also seek God's peace when we need it too. Thank you for responding in prayer when we call out to you! Knowing that you are crying out to God with us matters. You are all amazing.

Roosevelt continues to play the organ at church no matter how he is feeling. (He hasn't missed church service since being diagnosed on Sept. 7th.) And he continues to attend the boy's basketball games. He says, "I'm going to continue to have joy in this journey." Regularly, he will say "Lord, help me." Because that's what Fathers do...they help their children. And we can ask.

There is security for the One Who Trusts in the LORD...we know it to be true...
He who dwells in the shelter of the Most High
Will abide in the shadow of the Almighty.
I will say to the LORD, "My refuge and my fortress, My God, in whom I trust!" Psalm 91:1-3

Continue to pray for the Lord's healing...for the side effects to be lessened. That the Lord would continue to provide us strength and endurance for this war. We love you all!!
Bria Greenwood
Chandler Greenwood
Noah Javon Greenwood
Jacob Greenwood

There's going to be very painful moments in your life that will change your entire world in a matter of minutes. These moments will change YOU. Let them make you stronger, smarter, and kinder. But don't you go and become someone that your not. Cry. Scream if you have to. Then you straighten out that crown and keep it moving.

lessonslearnedinlife.com

 Like   Comment   Share

⭕🔵😊 **Michelle Mimi Davis and 433 others**

18 shares

Roosevelt's Reflection:

Well I can barely read this without crying. I am just being honest. I'm so thankful for Shay's words. I'm sure I have said this before but I will say it again. I'm thankful for my wife. I know she loves me unconditionally. She was helping me to maintain my perspective when my mind would run away with despairing thoughts. I knew that God had me, but I needed to hear his thoughts from Shay on a regular basis and still do. She calms me down.

Shay's Reflection:

There are so many nights that as darkness approached, I knew we were going to have a hard time going to sleep. If we did sleep, Roosevelt was going to wake up with a hot flash. When you have prostate cancer, you take hormone shots to get rid of the testosterone. Those hormone shots give you hot flashes, and it's not fun. I really didn't understand the impact that they have on people until Roosevelt started having them. He said that wanting to destroy things or hit something was the best way to describe it. I felt so bad for him. There were many things that we figured out to help us deal with waking up in the middle of the night and not being able to go back to sleep. We would listen to the Bible app read scripture to us, or we would watch funny videos through Facebook. We started following Christian comedians, which was always fun to see. Keeping our mind off our troubles, at night especially, was always the goal. Night time was the worse time for us. We were intentional about occupying our mind.

Shay Greenwood
January 26, 2017 · 🌐

⋯

Roosevelt's dad passed away 2 years ago. There isn't a day that goes by that he doesn't think about him and knows how his dad would be by his side during this trial. This special woman has fulfilled that role. Ozie was married to Roosevelt's dad for 15 years after his mom passed away. She is my husband's personal encourager now. 4 months ago, when Roosevelt was in the hospital, he said out loud to me how he wished his dad was there to encourage him. Within minutes, God sent Ozie into the hospital room. I was so thankful. She spoke the same words we know that his dad would have said. What an amazing God we serve that sees our need, and then supplies it so instantly!

Everyone needs a personal encourager, a person who loves you unconditionally, a person who speaks life into your life constantly, no matter what they may be going through...someone who prays out loud and calls out to God on your behalf. If you know her, you know what I'm talking about. We love and appreciate her so much!!

Roosevelt feels good today...looks good too, doesn't he?! We are praising God for who he is, what he has done, and what we know he will continue to do. (It confuses the enemy by the way.) THANK YOU for your prayers!!
#greenwoodstrong

👍 Like   💬 Comment   ↪ Share

👍❤️ Michelle Mimi Davis and 486 others

5 shares

Roosevelt's Reflection:

Whew! I can't get through the above post without crying: crying because I miss my dad, crying because of my situation, crying because I'm so thankful for this woman and what she meant to my dad, what she means to my family, and what she means to me. She would show up or call me when I needed encouragement the most. My son, Adam, who was 5 years old at the time of my diagnosis, mostly loved that she would bring Ginger Ale for me and cupcakes for him during my chemo treatments. Adam thought that both of them were for him, of course.

Shay's Reflection:

It would break my heart to hear Roosevelt's need to hear his father's voice. He missed him a lot. No one could encourage and speak life into your life like Roosevelt Greenwood, Sr., except his wife, Roosevelt's step-mom, Ozie.

I needed Ozie and anyone else to speak life into my husband. I could only say so much without sounding like a broken record. Roosevelt would often say to me, "You just have to say that because you are my wife," or "You just say that because you love me." Sometimes, you need to hear it from other people to believe it. The more encouragers for him, the better!!! We need others to surround us. We need a community. We need each other to make it through hard times. The joy of the Lord is our strength! (Nehemiah 8:10) We need people who are full of the Lord's joy and hope. Ozie is definitely that person who exudes joy, and it helped me so much to hear her words of encouragement to Roosevelt. She would often times use language and words just like Roosevelt's dad. It was familiar and comforting. I'm forever grateful to her.

Shay Greenwood
January 27, 2017 · 🌐

•••

This man. 😍 🖤
This smile is so fake, but full of faith!
I sent this picture to one of his BFFs that was checking on him and decided to post here. (with his permission 😜)
Today is the 3rd day after chemo.
And this afternoon became hard.
Thank God for basketball games...we get to watch 3 tonight‼️ Pray with us that he will make it through them.

Are there days when you are pushing through faking it?
In those moments, we can take our thoughts captive.
We have control.
We can choose to think on what is good.
Faith is knowing that it's all in God's hands and it can always be worse...those are **Roosevelt Greenwood**'s words just today.
All we need is the faith of a mustard seed.
A mustard seed is super tiny.
God meets us there. He gives it.
And it's enough.
That faith is the source of our joy...our strength.
Jesus came that we might have life and have it more abundantly.
He is present in our circumstances.
Never leaves.
It is how we keep going no matter what's going on with us and around us.
It's how you can smile regardless...even if it's fake at the time, down on the inside it's still full of faith and joy that only the Lord can provide.

#greenwoodstrong
#Jesusprovidesthepowertolivethislife
#cannothelpit

👍 Like   💬 Comment   ➤ Share

👍❤️ Michelle Mimi Davis and 473 others

7 shares

Roosevelt's Reflection:

As you can see, prayer is a very important part of our lives. We have had so many people praying for us, and I know that I wouldn't be doing as well as I am now if I didn't have my family and friends lifting me up in prayer. Days felt weary for me at times. My goal was to be well. I was thankful for the ability to attend events for my children. Amazingly, I wasn't feeling pain like I was in the beginning. I was able to wean off the pain medication I was on right after my last radiation treatment in November. I know that it was because people were praying.

Shay's Reflection:

Did you know that you can be sad and have joy at the same time? I remember complaining to my aunt about all the things going on in my life at this point. I was so sad for what we were experiencing and what Roosevelt had to go through.

Words from an old friend, Ms. who prayed boldly for us just a few nights later over the phone made such a huge difference. After praying, she said to us boldly: "Look up.
Life and death is in God's hands.
You can't do anything about that.
Keep the faith.
Do not fear.
I'm looking for God to heal you.
Say to yourself, "I shall not die, but live." (She didn't know Roosevelt Greenwood had been saying this from the beginning.)
God is not through with you yet.
Satan needs to keep his filthy hands off of you, in the name of Jesus!"

Prayer. It's the most important thing we can do on a daily basis. But, I often find it difficult to pray for myself or our situation. When I'm weary, I find myself saying, "Well, God knows." And, guess what? He does. I knew others were praying too. When we are weak, He is strong. I am thankful for the knowledge of that fact.

Chandler Greenwood is with **Roosevelt Greenwood** and **Shay Greenwood**.
January 29, 2017 · 👥

My mom is making my dad wear masks from now on 😌 we were in the ER early this morning because he had a fever, & it ends up that he has strep throat. He's taking antibiotics now...please pray that God heals him of this quickly! #greenwoodstrong

Make Profile Picture

❤️ Love   💬 Comment   ↗ Share

👍❤️😢 You, Michelle Mimi Davis and 480 others

1 share

Roosevelt's Reflection:

"In sickness and in health." I didn't realize this would come so soon. Shay and I had only been married 21 years, and I have to burden my family with taking care of me instead of the other way around. In the picture above, I had just left the emergency room because my immune system was low and my white blood cells were not fighting hard enough, so I ended up with a fever. I love, love, love my wife. She reads everything about my diagnosis and knows the symptoms of the things I will go through or could go through. From another time, I knew her routine when I didn't feel the best. I heard her search for the thermometer. When she found it, I knew that in a few seconds, it was going to be in my mouth. Of to the hospital we went. It was a different day, but the same routine on this day. This was my life, and it was hard.

Shay's Reflection:

When you are taking chemotherapy, your white blood cell count lowers, and you are susceptible to catching a cold or the flu easily. This was that time. I never hesitated if Roosevelt had a fever. I was told if he had a fever, to call the doctor. I called the doctor, and they said to come to the ER. Here we were fighting cancer, and I was not going to have him die because of a fever from an infection of some sort! I know I can't control anything, but at least as a caregiver, I was going to do my part. He didn't want to wear the masks. But I was determined that we were going to at least do what we know to do.

Shay Greenwood
February 9, 2017 · 🌐

For me...This represents the enemy being defeated! 💥
Boom ba-by! 💥
These two spots were so cluttered.
I hadn't dealt with a lot on my desk (personal and business) because it seemed too hard and I was handling so much already. You couldn't even see the desktop.
My life hasn't changed, but these spaces have.
I feel like I can exhale.
I feel like I have control.
I feel like I can think more clearly.
And I thank God He gives us a little slice of something that we can be in charge of and make decisions on.
I have more to make decisions on and my goal is March 30th

to play catch up. It took 5 months to get things out of order...and I gave myself 90 days to take this part of my life back so my mind can be at REST (my word for the year).

What in your life do you need to take back? Pick one thing. Google the steps and start today!! Don't overthink it. The results will be like a little heaven on earth.
#greenwoodstrong

👍 Like   💬 Comment   ↪ Share

🔵🔵 Michelle Mimi Davis and 212 others

1 share

Shay's Reflection:

Trust me, I know that I have no control over anything. When things seem out of control though, I love to clean and feel like I have some control. If things can't be nice and neat in my life, then I can at least have my house nice and neat for a day. When you are going through a new normal in your life because of life circumstances outside of your control, it feels especially heavy and hard when everything around you is a hot mess, too. Cleaning this day helped me rid that feeling of things being out of control. I ruled the day that day!

As I look at my bed, I can't help but think about my sweet, dear friends, Jan & Chelsey, who orchestrated getting a new mattress and bedding for us. Even before Roosevelt's diagnosis, he would talk about how difficult it was to sleep on our mattress. (In retrospect, it could have been the cancer lesions on his spine causing the difficulty sleeping.) After he was diagnosed and we were in the hospital, Jan & Chelsey picked me up for an outing to get away from the hospital. I didn't realize that they had gathered money from my Premier Designs team and other girlfriends in the business in order for me to purchase a new mattress and bedding before Roosevelt came home from the hospital. It was the best gift ever. All I wanted was for him to experience some comfort when he came home. And, these friends, who were like family, fulfilled that dream for me. What an amazing group of friends we have!

Chandler Greenwood is with **Roosevelt Greenwood** and **Shay Greenwood**.
February 11, 2017 ·

Whew my parents look GOOD. 😍 🔥

So thankful that Jesus gave me parents who are full of faith and are a constant example of people living a life completely trusting the Lord even in the midst of the hardest circumstances, believing that His plan for our lives is absolutely perfect, & knowing that He is sovereign over all things no matter what.

#greenwoodstrong

Roosevelts reflection:

When I look at this picture, I see a very different version of myself, I was bloated, and I had gained probably 30 pounds. The chemotherapy, according to my doc, had stripped away my metabolism, and I couldn't really burn any calories. My self esteem was at an all time low. I used to think that I was a fairly good looking guy, but I didn't feel that way. People told me that I looked good, but I believed that they were just being nice. Despite how I felt about how I looked, I was thankful for life.

Shay's Reflection:

In this picture, we were on our way to a church Anniversary dinner celebration for Jonathan and Renata. Roosevelt and Jonathan were family friends, and Jonathan asked us to speak about marriage at the dinner. As I look back on this picture, I remember Chandler saying that we should take a picture. But, honestly, neither one of us was up for taking the picture. I was tired and the picture shows it. I couldn't find a true smile. We took the picture, I'm sure, several times and this was the best we could do. It makes me laugh now. I know how I felt when we took the picture. "Just hurry up and take the picture." BUT, I'm also thankful for the memory of how the Lord was carrying us regardless of our feelings.

Shay Greenwood
February 27, 2017 · 🌐

Last Tuesday, I took this picture as we drove to Lake Cormorant, MS. **Roosevelt Greenwood** and I went to our son Noah's playoff game. (GHS ended up losing in the 1st round. It was a great season and they fought hard.) I love how we can see God in everything (if we look for Him, if we want to see Him).

This picture reminds me of the scripture Psalm 19:1 that says, "The heavens declare the glory of God, and the sky above proclaims his handiwork." Nature will always remind us that there is a God. I'm so thankful for those reminders. I need them. We all need them.

I love how the storms of life teach us so many things IF we are willing to listen.
We tend to pay more attention during storms.

We are staying the night in the hospital because Roosevelt had a fever of 102.
His immune system was low because of the chemo he received on Wednesday.
He started having cold symptoms Thursday.
(Adam and I had colds...Still left in the house obviously.)
Fever started Sunday around 7...
He doesn't have the flu.
It was negative.
His white blood count is low.
They are pumping him with antibiotics.
And just being careful.

I find myself asking God...continue to speak to me through this...speak to us through this...not necessarily audibly...just want to see with spiritual eyes.
I want to have the Lord's perspective through this.
God knows where we are.
He hasn't left us.
We know he is faithful.
We know we can trust Him.
And He proves that He's here...
✓ Through a nurse "Ann" who is a 7 year uterine cancer survivor and she shared her story...
✓ Through our transporter from the ER to our hospital room

"Tom" who saw us holding hands and asked if we had just gotten married and shared his story of his recent divorce...

✔ Through the security guard "Joe" who walked me from the parking garage and who told me that we are in the end days and that's why the weather is crazy...and you have to live each day as if it's your last...thanks Joe. 😌

You were created by God.
For His glory.
For His pleasure.
For His purposes.
We are called to live for Him and not for ourselves.
We are called to live a life poured out for Him.
Jesus alone is the answer.
We are so grateful that He is how we are able to withstand the storms of life. We may get wet, (thanks **Rob Futral** for that picture) but we know without a shadow of a doubt that we have a Great Navigator who helps us to be calm (even though it can be scary) and strengthen us when we feel tired and weak.

We will forever praise You, Lord!
Thank You for being here and allowing us to see You.
#greenwoodstrong

🤍 Like   💬 Comment   ↗ Share

👍❤️ Michelle Mimi Davis and 121 others

97

Roosevelt's Reflection:

I'm lying in the hospital bed, and the chemotherapy has taken its toll on my body. I tell people all the time that if it wasn't for Shay, I would be with Jesus now because I was sleeping in bed at home and as usual out of nowhere a thermometer is in my mouth and I have a 102 fever. Now if it was just me I would have taken some Tylenol and just sleep it off, but nooo super woman to the rescue and she doesn't take no for an answer. My oncologist is at the hospital to see me he has never come to any of my hospital stays so something must be seriously wrong. My doc just informed me that he was going to stop the treatments because my body couldn't take anymore. Ok Lord I'm ready if its my time to go, I'm not afraid I win either way this goes, I don't want to leave my family, but I'm ready.

Shay's Reflection:

One of the songs that became an anthem for the both of us during our very first hospital stay is called "For Your Glory" by Tasha Cobbs. Some of the lyrics are:

Lord if I
Find favor in Your sight
Lord please
Hear my hearts cry
I'm desperately waiting
To be where You are
I'll cross the hottest desert
I'll travel near or far
For Your glory
I will do anything

Just to see You
To behold You as my King
For Your glory
I will do anything
Just to see you
To behold You as my King
Songwriters: Mia Santai Booker

I would encourage you to listen to Tasha Cobbs sing it. Check it out on YouTube. There is nothing like giving your life to Jesus and being in His presence. Unfortunately, we feel that presence mostly in the dark times of life.

I thought that this is just the way our journey would be: hospital stays and treatments with a Stage 4 diagnosis. It just plain sucked. I told myself that since I was going through this, I could add the word "sucked" to my vocabulary. Cancer sucks. Treatments sucked. Staying in hospital sucked. But, you know what? What could I do about it but go with the flow? I could wallow in the suckiness (I made that word up), or, I could choose to have joy no matter my circumstances. I firmly believe that it's okay to feel all the feels. You can feel sad over your situation. AND, you can feel blessed. Whatever you focus on grows. I may not always get it right, but my goal is always to choose joy no matter how hard things are around me.

God promises in Isaiah 43:2, "When you go through deep waters, I will be with you." He is faithful. We can trust Him. He will always be with you. Say that over and over again until you believe it. It's definitely hard, but it's a mindset and heartset we need to practice to live this life successfully.

Shay Greenwood
March 2, 2017

Update: Thank you for praying for my sweet husband and our family. He is getting better day by day. Because of the chemo treatment last week, his white blood count was low and he had a viral infection. He had a fever of 102 and they admitted him to pump him with antibiotics. They gave him a shot to increase his white blood count and that's increasing day by day. The side effects of that are bad bone pain, but that's subsiding day by day.

We had a tough 4 days, but God.
There were tears and sadness.
This journey is hard.
But we still have a joy and a peace that only God can provide.

Roosevelt will ask me just to hear my answer...
"How did I get cancer?"
"Because God said to satan, "Have you considered my servant, Roosevelt?"
That's a line from Job 1:8...where "The Lord said to Satan, Have you considered My servant Job? For there is no one like him on the earth, a blameless and upright man, fearing God and turning away from evil."

I believe this for my husband too.
In sadness, Job worshipped the Lord.
And we will do the same.
4-ever, no matter what.

Job 1:20-22 says: Then Job arose and tore his robe and shaved his head, and he fell to the ground and worshiped. He said, Naked I came from my mother's womb, and Naked I shall return there. The Lord gave and the Lord has taken away. Blessed be the name of the Lord. Through all this Job did not sin nor did he blame God.

We love the Lord.
Life is hard.
And, we can trust Him. 🖤
#greenwoodstrong

100

THOUGH HE SLAY ME, YET WILL I TRUST HIM.

~ JOB (13:15)

👍 Like   💬 Comment   ↪ Share

👍😊😢 Michelle Mimi Davis and 452 others

12 shares

Roosevelt's Reflection:

Shay compares my story to Job's story. I cringe when I hear her say that because the Bible says that he was blameless, upright, fearing God, and turning away from evil. That's a tall task that I believe I fall short, nevertheless, it lifts my spirit to know that you don't have to do bad things for bad things to happen to you. From time to time, I wondered if I was being punished for something I did in the past? I can hold on to Job saying God is just, and I can only hope my story will turn out like Job 42:12. The Lord blessed the latter days of Job more than his beginning. That's what I'm holding on too.

Shay's Reflection:

Roosevelt constantly questioned what he was going through, what we were going through, and I became really good at answering his questions. Not in an irritated way, but answering him knowing that he just wanted to hear me say the truth. I would continue to speak the truth to him over and over again. It was so good for me to hear it, too.

Shay Greenwood
April 6, 2017 · 🌐

We couldn't sleep last night because of this.
Chandler Greenwood was chosen by this "men's club" on Mississippi College's campus as their freshman "Sweetheart". I guess it's a huge deal. It's the sweetest gift from God after such a hard first year in college, having to be away from home, when all she wanted to do was be snuggled next to us during **Roosevelt Greenwood**'s treatments especially. They have watched her and chose her. It's the picture of who Jesus is in our lives. He is always there watching and seeing everything we do. Always present. Always there. He chooses us. Unlike this though, the invitation is open to everyone, we don't have to do anything but accept His invitation into our lives.

These boys said incredibly sweet things about her...they were watching her unaware. God is always there even when you don't feel like He sees. In no way am I saying that these boys are God. But, sometimes, when you have had a tough year...it feels awesome to know that someone noticed and chose you to represent the devotion you have to God's will in your life...even though it's hard. What an honor! So excited for this girl. God's plans for you are perfect. Can't quit school now, girl! (Sorry, not sorry, to put you on blast

about quitting.)
#builtinsecurity
#daddysaidtheybetterprotecther
#greenwoodstrong

👍 Like   💬 Comment   ↪ Share

⭕💙😮 Michelle Mimi Davis and 403 others

3 shares

Roosevelt's Reflection:

As a Dad, you feel like you should be strong and show no weaknesses. It is what I saw and experienced as a young man growing up. My Dad didn't show any emotions like being sad, or crying; it was non-existent. This post makes me think about my children and makes me wonder what they think about what's going on with me. Prior to my diagnosis, I didn't show much emotions ever, but since my diagnosis, I now show a lot of emotions. I get overwhelmed just thinking about Shay and the children. God is faithful, and he sees me where I am. I now know that emotions are part of life. Jesus wept and he is my example.

These boys have blessed me in more ways than one. We were able to purchase a home just a year ago in February 2018. It's hard to ask your friends to help you move. Not only have they been there to support, encourage, and pray for Chandler the first year of my diagnosis, but they also helped my family move our furniture from our rental home of 5 years into our new home. I will always be grateful for their love for Chandler and my family.

Shay's Reflection:

What an amazing example of God supplying what we need! Chandler was so consumed with what was going on with Roosevelt that she felt alone on campus. She tried going through the Rush process, but didn't feel like it was "her". She would call and text us to ask about Roosevelt's progress. She wanted to attend all of his doctor's appointments and in her mind, school was in the way. She spent a lot of time alone because she wasn't going through Rush. This was just what she needed to help re-engage her with God's will for her life. Her major is Worship Leadership. What a perfect fit for her and her musical talents! God wanted her to keep going and knew this would be the perfect thing for her. What young lady wouldn't want 60 young men – brothers, as Chandler calls them - thinking about you? It fulfilled her need for fellowship and community on campus and lessened her thoughts about what was going on with Roosevelt.

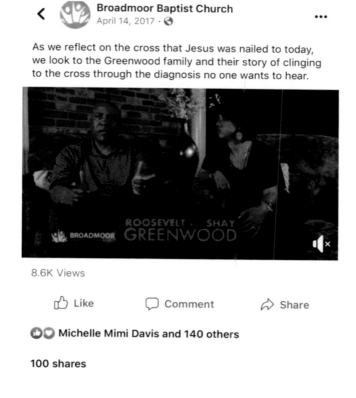

Broadmoor Baptist Church
April 14, 2017 · 🌐

As we reflect on the cross that Jesus was nailed to today, we look to the Greenwood family and their story of clinging to the cross through the diagnosis no one wants to hear.

ROOSEVELT ·· SHAY
BROADMOOR GREENWOOD

8.6K Views

👍 Like   💬 Comment   ↪ Share

👍❤️ Michelle Mimi Davis and 140 others

100 shares

Our reflection:

We will continuously praise the Lord for what he has done for us! This video depicts His faithfulness. We are forever thankful for how He has brought us to this point. We will cling to the cross always and forever!

We are beyond grateful for our Broadmoor family who went above and beyond to come alongside us in so many ways.

 Shay Greenwood is with **Roosevelt Greenwood** and **26 others.**
April 22, 2017 · 🌐

What an incredible day this was for our family! **Lauren Worthey Swanson**...and so many others who volunteered with her...Thank you isn't enough for the love we felt today! The amount of work that is put into something like this did not go unnoticed. You blessed us more than you can even imagine! Thank you to those that came to walk or run, and those who donated! We have the best friends and family ever and we wouldn't want to walk this journey without you! We love and appreciate you! You have made this season easier to walk through and easier to keeping fighting. We are stronger together.
Love,
Roosevelt and Shay
#greenwoodstrong

Like   Comment   Share

Michelle Mimi Davis and 231 others

1 share

 Shay Greenwood
April 22, 2017 · 🌐

#rallyforRoosevelt
#greenwoodstrong

 Michelle Mimi Davis and 179 others   5 Comments

Roosevelt's Reflection:

Being vulnerable does not come easy to me, so throughout this process, I struggled with accepting generosity from others. My friend Blake has known about my condition since the very beginning when we thought it was a sciatic nerve injury. We used to sit at the boys' football practice, and I would ask him what he thought was going on with my leg because I was having pain, and my calf was starting to atrophy. Blake is very smart and he would often give me advice on things I could do to strengthen the calf and exercises I could do to strengthen my back, which could give me some relief from the pain I was experiencing.

After finding out that my pain was from a more serious condition, Blake's beautiful, sweet wife, Lauren, wanted to do something for us so she organized a fundraiser in the form of a race, and the proceeds would be given to us to help with our medical expenses. What you see in this picture is a community of people coming to our rescue; some weren't pictured. Why would people, many whom we knew and many whom we did not know, show such kindness? It is totally overwhelming and we are so thankful for each one of you.

Shay's Reflection:

Just a few days before this, Roosevelt was in the hospital. It was a weary time for me. It was thoughtful things like this event that truly kept me going. My sister Michelle and her family and my sweet friend Cathy and her family came from out of town to run in the race. There were so many friends and family locally that came. Lauren and so many others who helped her blessed our lives by planning an event for Roosevelt and our family, and we will forever be grateful!!

Shay Greenwood
May 5, 2017 · 🌐

This is one of those Romans 8:28 moments.
"And we know that God causes ALL things to work together for good to those who love God, to those who are called according to His purpose."

God promotes us to 5 diamond in the middle of difficult circumstances, so **Roosevelt Greenwood** can say this...on stage, in front of people. It's the last place he wants to be.

This man is full of courage and full of faith.
I'm so proud of how he is allowing God to use him.
He is a walking miracle and we will not take that for granted.
What Satan meant for bad, God means for good.
God is good no matter what!
To God be the glory for the things He has done!

#godsgrace
#godpromotes
#greenwoodstrong
#Histimingisperfect
#wecantrustHim
#waitonHim

2.7K Views

👍 Like   💬 Comment   ↗ Share

👍❤️😮 Michelle Mimi Davis and 307 others

11 shares

109

Roosevelt's Reflection:

Most people don't realize that I'm shy and never want to be on stage or have the light shined on me. Since I've been on this journey, I've been forced to step outside my comfort zone more and more. This is an example of how God was giving me an opportunity to share my testimony and thank so many others for praying for us. Because we had promoted another level in our business, we were introduced on stage. And, because we had to introduce ourselves, we were able to give glory to God for what he had been doing in our lives since the diagnosis and every one of us praised God for it.

Shay's Reflection:

This was our annual leadership trip with Premier Designs High Fashion Jewelry. Premier is the direct sales company that I have been a distributor with for 19 years. My business was definitely a highlight for me especially in the hardest times in my life, especially during this time. Serving and enriching the lives of others helped me to not focus on my own troubles so much. I love the scripture from Proverbs 11:25 that says, "The generous man will be prosperous, And he who waters will himself be watered." It was such a blessing to be able to get out of the house and be with "just the girls" at jewelry parties or help a client with her wardrobe. It was a way for me to take care of myself and have connections outside of our normal day to day battle with treatments or how Roosevelt was feeling that day.

We were celebrated on stage because of our promotion to 5 Diamond Designer. At that time, it meant that we have 150 people on our team. We were so thankful for our team and how hard they worked to get us to that place. It was a time for celebration, for sure, and we were amazed at all that God had done up to this place.

One of the highlights from this trip was having one of my friends, Pauline, text me just before we were going to leave for the airport to go back home. I stood in awe. What she didn't know was that Roosevelt had just started having pain in his hip. At this point, we were 7 months out from Roosevelt having radiation to his spine and hips and it was concerning. Our immediate reaction ALWAYS is "Is the cancer spreading?" Roosevelt was in so much pain from it that it was hard to walk up and down stairs. We really didn't know how he was going to make it to the hotel and through the airport. I was already anticipating getting a wheelchair. We didn't have any pain pills with us. He hadn't had pain in his body in months. Then, I received the text from Pauline. She wanted to pray with us before we left. And, she was persistent. Thankfully.

We met her in the lobby outside this conference room. We sat on the couches and we told her that we thought it was pretty amazing that she texted. Roosevelt needed prayer for his pain. We prayed. And, the short story? Roosevelt was healed from that pain in that instant. He had no more pain from that day to this present day. It brings tears to my eyes just writing that. We believe in prayer. We believe that God answers prayer. We believe that prayers can be answered in an instant. Sometimes those answers are not now. Sometimes those answers are no. That day, we received a yes. We were stronger for it. Thank you, Pauline, for hearing from the Lord like you do.

Shay Greenwood
May 14, 2017 · 🌐

🐝Happy Mom's Day to all my momma friends!! 🐝
For 21 years, God has blessed me to hold precious children in my lap. Even though my nature is to be cleaning something, or working, or doing something "more productive" (because ain't nobody got time to just sit around), God has shown me that there is no greater "productivity" than pouring into the lives of our 5 children. What a blessing it has been.
What amazing truths God has revealed to ME as I talk with them, especially when God points His finger at me and says, "and what about you? Are you doing that? Are you being a good example?" Ugh...so hard to hear those truths from your Heavenly Father as you are trying to teach somebody, something! 😜

We all need grace to make it.
I thank God for His grace.
Who needs a little grace today?
Chill, Little Momma friends, and know that you are a great mom and that you are loved! 🖤

Thank you to my children who make life real, who constantly bring a better perspective to it. I think my dream day is to be alone, in a hammack, on the beach, with a book.
That day would be like heaven.
But this baby-holding momma day is better. God knows it is. And, I'm grateful for the gift of being a mom. I will never take this role for granted.

#greenwoodstrong
#reallife

👍 Like   💬 Comment   ➢ Share

👍❤️😊 Michelle Mimi Davis and 208 others

1 share

Roosevelt's Reflection:

Moms, you guys rock, nothing like the love of a
mother.

> *Proverbs 31:25-30: She is clothed with strength
> and dignity; she can laugh at the days to come.
> 26 She speaks with wisdom, and faithful
> instruction is on her tongue. 27 She watches
> over the affairs of her household and does not
> eat the bread of idleness. 28 Her children arise*

and call her blessed; her husband also, and he praises her. 29 Many women do noble things, but you surpass them all." 30 Charm is deceptive, and beauty is fleeing; but a woman who fears the LORD is to be praised.

This description is Shay and I'm so blessed that she belongs to me.

Shay's Reflection:

There were times in this journey that I felt so tired and exhausted from taking care of EVERYTHING. That's just how you feel. I didn't want to be strong all the time. And, I wanted to give up sometimes. But, I knew that the feeling would pass. I just needed a break to focus on the good things going on in my life. I had to count my blessings one by one. Some days I had a pity party and couldn't think of any good things. And, other days, I could keep my thoughts captive and push through to another day. I had to be okay with not being okay. It's normal. It's a part of my life. My mind went to: Philippians 4:8 which says: Finally, brethren, whatever is true, whatever is honorable, whatever is right, whatever is pure, whatever is lovely, whatever is of good repute, if there is any excellence and if anything worthy of praise, dwell on these things." No matter how messy my house got, no matter how I was feeling, I had to force myself to dwell on what was good in my life.

Shay Greenwood
May 31, 2017 · 🌐

Scan results: "No cancer...still in remission..." After we stopped holding our breath, it sounded like the heavens opened up and music came flooding into the room! 🎺🎺🎺🎺🎺🎺

Have you ever felt rescued? That's how we feel today. We feel like the Lord has sustained us and that He has rescued us.

It is heartbreaking to read the Facebook posts on the prostate cancer support groups of how horrible this disease is: How it changes lives, provides tremendous heartache, and ruins families and marriages. We remain in awe over what we get to experience through this, and what we have been rescued from and we are so thankful!

The fight continues...thank you for your texts, calls and constantly praying!!!!!
#greenwoodstrong Roosevelt Greenwood

Roosevelt's Reflection:

Thank you Jesus. I Corinthians 15: 57 But thanks be to God who give us the victory through our Lord Jesus Christ.

Shay's Reflection:

Good news is amazing to receive, and we were so thankful to receive it. We were living a new normal life. The Prostate Cancer support groups were so raw about what men and their families were going through. Like I said before, I would read them so I could anticipate what may come next being careful that I wouldn't take their feelings and emotions on myself. It was heartbreaking to read some of their stories. Many stories were difficult to read, but I knew I wanted to know as much as I could. There were many times that I could calm Roosevelt's fears knowing that what he was experiencing was normal. I could also calm my own fears knowing what to expect and to help both of us to put things into perspective.

What people don't realize is that prostate cancer, and other cancers, can strip away the patient's marriage and family. Roosevelt is on daily chemo pills called Zytiga. He also takes a hormone shot called Trelstar. He also take Insulin twice a day and is on a few high blood pressure pills. Prostate cancer is driven by testosterone and the hormone shot lowers your testosterone to zero. The side effects of the hormone shot have affected Roosevelt and our sex life the most. We wanted to be real about that because we both have had to grieve in our own way about that. It's hard, and it's not the life we expected at our age. It's funny how we have switched roles in who the aggressor is. This is part of our new normal and one of the many depths that true love requires. We will end here so that our children aren't too embarrassed!

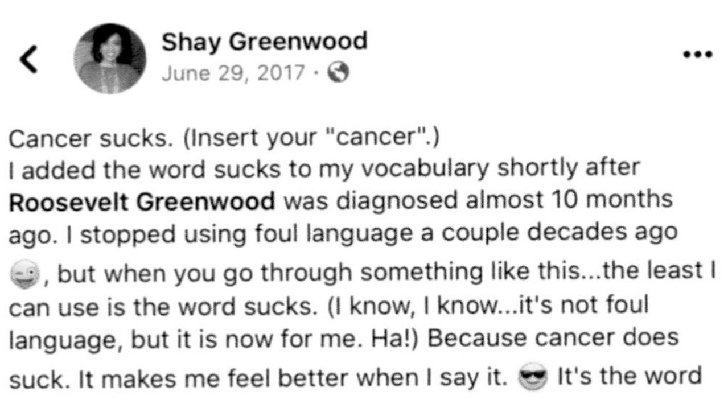

Shay Greenwood
June 29, 2017 ·

Cancer sucks. (Insert your "cancer".)
I added the word sucks to my vocabulary shortly after **Roosevelt Greenwood** was diagnosed almost 10 months ago. I stopped using foul language a couple decades ago 😜, but when you go through something like this...the least I can use is the word sucks. (I know, I know...it's not foul language, but it is now for me. Ha!) Because cancer does suck. It makes me feel better when I say it. 😎 It's the word

that best describes it.

I worked out at 5:10 this morning and during my workout I felt emotional. At first I thought, I must be sleepy...I'm not a morning person. Then, I thought about why I'm working out in the first place...Because cancer sucks... It sucks the life out of caregivers. Support group pages are overwhelmed with caregivers who's health declines because they aren't taking care of themselves. So that's why I started working out consistently in January...after gaining 10 pounds, I knew I had to do something different. And while I should be happy that I can even exercise in the first place...And taking care of your health is a great thing...It makes me sad to think how we got to this place...

But God.
Seriously.
I can go down this road of sadness and despair.
And, then God takes me to the many things He has done through this very hard journey.
I thank God for His word..."it's right all by itself" my father in love use to say. I thank God for His Holy Spirit that reminds

God is who He says He is.
We found out between last night and today. Two close friend's family/friend like family passed away.
Our reminder: This is not our home.

I have to focus my thoughts on what's good right now...

✓ Financial provision in times of need...too many times to name.

✓ Roosevelt's remission...people find it weird that the doctor would even call it that when its incurable. I count this as a miracle. (Medically they expect him to become hormone resistant one day...we pray otherwise!!) He has more good days than bad days. Thank you, Lord! The bad days remind us of where we have been.

✓ Children who haven't skipped a beat...dreams being realized...we are thankful for what God has provided rather than what we think we wanted in fulfilling those dreams.

✓ An AMAZING tribe of support and encouragement. (Really no words can express our gratefulness for what you have done for our family.)

✓ A house to live in, cars to drive in.

✓ The wisdom of medical staff.

I could go on and on. But this is what comes to mind today to help me to take my throughts captive.

This world is not our home.
Don't settle in.
Live your life in that light.
You have this life, with these circumstances...
Now, how are you going to live?

What are you going to do about it?
How are you going to honor God?
How are you going to represent Jesus?
How are you going to stay encouraged?
How are you going to take care of yourself and others around you?
How are you going to live at peace knowing that you serve a great Big God who can do exceedingly, abundantly above all that you can ask or think?

Be encouraged.
He has you in the palm of His hand and nothing can come to you but through His fingers of love.
Better days are coming!
That's our hope.
#greenwoodstrong

Roosevelt's Reflection:

When I read this post, I asked the question again, "How did I get cancer?" This is a very real question for me. What stands out for me is that the doctors said that I can become "hormone resistant". I take a hormone shot every 3 months. What they were saying is that my body could start rejecting the medicine that helps to keep my PSA numbers low. That's an overwhelming thought for me. The next question I have is, then what? What happens then? Does the cancer keep growing and consume my body? Then I started thinking about seeing my mom and dad in their last days when they were dying of cancer. These are normal thoughts for me. But, I don't like staying in or going to that place. I like to think of happy thoughts. So, I focused my mind on the promises of God. I've asked the Lord to allow me to be around for "3 scores and 10," which is 70 years in the bible. My faith helps me to believe that this is so. I'm determined to see my children get married, have grandchildren, and all the good things that we all expect to see.

Shay's Reflection:

Cancer does suck. There is no way around it. And, God is still good. That's the truth of our situation. I

119

remember someone telling us that we make cancer look good. I know that sounds like a crazy thought. What that means to me is that we make God look good despite our circumstances, and I take that as a compliment. Even though we have bad days, the Lord is how we are able to still smile, still get up, and still get dressed. The joy of the Lord has been our constant strength.

Shay Greenwood is with **Roosevelt Greenwood** and **22 others**.

July 22, 2017 · Fort Worth, TX · 🌐

Remember my troubles before my trip?! Crazy how I was so close to saying "Forget it, I'm not going." When you deal with 10 months of trauma, you can get to a place afterward where any little thing can be the straw that breaks the camels back. All I kept doing last week, as things were falling a part, is put one foot in front of the other and just get to Ft. Worth the best way I could!! 😄 I kept praying and did the next thing over and over again.

All these people plus so many more inspired me to keep pressing my way. 17 years of going to this conference...I knew it would bless us!! This time it was beyond what I could imagine or think. Thank you, Lord for what you have done...And thank you for an amazing community of people in which to live this life! #toGodbetheglory #teamshiningstar #greenwoodstrong

Roosevelt's Reflection:

This conference is one conference that we have attended for the last 17 years, and I usually look forward to going, but I didn't this year because I felt like all eyes would be on me. My appearance had changed. I knew people would have questions. I just didn't want to be in big crowds. Each year, they give out awards for Senior Leaders. Shay's name was called for one of them, and I couldn't stop the tears from flowing. The hormone shot always had me so emotional. I don't like crying. I was so happy for Shay, though, and so thankful to Premier for seeing what I see in her. She is my personal encourager, especially when I feel depressed. She constantly knows the right things to say. She knows God's word and is able to share with me what the Bible says. For her to receive this award was spot on. Not only is she like this for me, but I know that she is like this for so many others. In marriage, we don't always get it right, but, I thank God that I got it right with Shay. She is the love of my life, and I appreciate her so much. Words can't even express what she is to me.

Shay's Reflection:

We have been reps in Premier Designs for 19 years. What a blessing it has been to be able to be a stay at home/homeschool mom all of that time! The company was founded on biblical principles and has always been a way for me to be able to have a life outside of my family life. During this cancer journey, I was able to enrich the lives of others, and it really gave me something else to focus on.

This trip was such a blessing for us in so many ways. We were able to step outside of the day to day life at home. We needed a break. We were able to see our team and friends like family from across the country. And, surprisingly, I was awarded "The Marge Caldwell Encourager of the Year Award" from the company. After all that I had been through over the last several months, I couldn't believe it when my name was called. Roosevelt cried like a baby. He was happy for me of course. But it was also the hormone shots!

Shay Greenwood
December 1, 2017 · 🌐

You sometimes question when you read "Always be Joyful" when cancer is a part of your life. You question it especially when you get a diagnosis or when you are slapped in the face with "Your PSA numbers are increasing...this is Stage 4 cancer...it's not curable...so we go on to the next treatment."

Those were the words that the doctor said to us yesterday at the monthly regular checkup.

Cancer doesn't make you Joyful. God does. 🙌

Roosevelt Greenwood's PSA was .09 back in November 2016 and now it's at .53 last month...for the last three months it has been trending upward and that's not what you want (although it's in a normal range).

Every fiber of my being says to not tell you because it hurts too bad to write it. But a relative said, "Keep doing what you did before." Another friend said, "That perfect plan He designed before Rosie was born, is still in effect."

We are soliciting your prayers that this next treatment will suppress the PSA level and that Roosevelt experiences minimal side effects. (He will take Zytiga daily which is in a pill form.)

Did you know that you can be sad and still have joy?? Joy comes from the Lord and when we focus on who God says He is. ...these are the words from Priscilla Shirer that come to me this morning...it's long but worth the read. And I will that only God can provide.

Through tears, you can be sad about your circumstances as you rejoice in all that God is in your life. We have so many things to be thankful for...too many to count.
#greenwoodstrong
#mengetyourPSAchecked
Bria Greenwood Chandler Greenwood Noah Javon Greenwood Jacob Greenwood

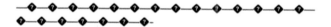

He is the first and the last, the beginning and the end. He's the keeper of creation and the creator of all. He's the architect of the universe and the manager of all time. He always was, always is, always will be unmoved, unchanged, undefeated and never undone.

He was bruised but brought healing, He was pierced but eased pain, He was persecuted but brought freedom, He was dead and brings life. He is risen to bring power and He reigns to bring peace.

The world can't understand Him, armies can't defeat Him, schools can't explain Him and leaders – they can't ignore

Him. Herrod couldn't kill Him, Nero couldn't crush Him, the new age cannot replace Him and Oprah cannot explain Him away.You remind yourself, that He is light, He is love, He is longevity and He is the Lord. He is goodness and kindness and faithfulness and He is God. He is holy and righteousness and powerful and pure.His ways are right, His

He's our Savior, our guide, our peace, our joy, our comfort, our Lord and He rules our lives.I serve Him because....His bond is love, His yoke is easy, His burden is light and His goal for us is abundant life. I follow Him because He's the wisdom of the wise, the power of the powerful, the ancient of days, the ruler of rulers, the leader of all leaders. His goal is a relationship with me.He'll never leave you, never forsake you, never mislead you, never forget you, never overlook you, and never cancel your appointment in his appointment book.When you fall He'll lift you up. When you fail, he'll forgive you. When you're weak, He's strong. When you're lost, He's your way. When you're afraid, He's your courage.When you stumble, he will steady you. When you're hurt He's gonna heal you. When you're broken, He will mend you. When you're blind, He will lead you. When you're hungry, He will feed you. When you face trials, He's with you. When I face persecution, He shields me. When I face problems, He will comfort me. When I face loss, He will provide for me. And when we face death, He will carry us all home to meet Him.He is everything, for everybody, everywhere, every time and in everyway. He is your God. And that sisters, is who you belong to.Anointed, Transformed & Redeemed 2008 - Priscilla Shirer

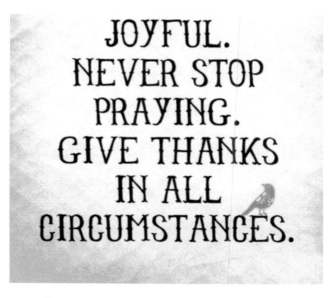

JOYFUL.
NEVER STOP
PRAYING.
GIVE THANKS
IN ALL
CIRCUMSTANCES.

👍 Like   💬 Comment   ↪ Share

👍❤️😢 Precious Alai and 268 others

9 shares

Roosevelt's Reflection:

Cancer takes you through so many peaks and valleys, and this was a valley for me. Hearing that my PSA was going back up hurt me. All the medicine that I was taking to lower my PSA was not working. I needed an additional med to try to keep my numbers low. I was told that the chemo oral med that was being prescribed would help to get my numbers back to zero. I wasn't happy about having to take more chemo and what it was actually doing to my body. Of course, I had all these thoughts and questions, but I knew that I had to take the medication to stay alive and prolong my life. I wanted to do what I had to do to be with my family.

Shay's Reflection:

It was devastating to get the news that we were going to the next treatment. When Roosevelt was first diagnosed, Dr. Qu listed the possible treatments that Roosevelt could get if the PSA numbers went back up, we were still devastated. We didn't like it and we were sad. And, we were hopeful that the next treatment would work. Dr. Qu wanted the next treatment to be immunotherapy. We were shocked when the insurance company said no. They basically told us that Roosevelt wasn't sick enough. It makes me so angry when I think about the things that insurance companies decide on. I constantly had to ask the Lord to help me to be patient and rely upon his guidance and strength for issues like this. I wondered how people who don't do their research deal with all the insurance issues that come up.

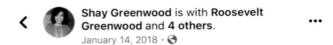

<   **Shay Greenwood** is with **Roosevelt Greenwood** and **4 others.**   •••
January 14, 2018 · 🌐

Even when life is messy and sometimes downright difficult, there are very special moments in life that make every single second of hard oh so worth it.

"I could have no greater joy than to hear that my children live in the truth. 3 John 4
#broadmoorbaptistchurch
#greenwoodstrong

January 14, 2018: Deacon Roosevelt Greenwood, Broadmoor Baptist Church

Roosevelt's Reflection:

Church is very important to me. I grew up a Preacher's kid and had been in church my entire life. I had served at Church as a musician but never as a Deacon. It was such an honor to be asked to be a Deacon at Broadmoor. I had never considered being a Deacon until now. Unfortunately, after serving for a few months, I had to give up the role because any time there were responsibilities or events to attend, I couldn't attend because of being ill or too fatigued.

This picture was taken during the ordination, and it was such a special time. My children gathered and prayed for me. Not only did they pray, but other friends came and prayed over us. It was a special moment that I will never forget.

Shay's Reflection:

What a precious, precious time, and it was really unexpected! Roosevelt was nominated to be a Deacon at our church. It wasn't something he thought about at all. It was something that was a blessing, though, because he had a heart to serve especially considering how he had been served over the past several months. When they told him that he was nominated, he decided that it would be awesome to serve others and pay how he was served forward. We had talked about how good it felt to be able to bless others like we have been blessed. Not that we weren't doing this before, but we now wanted it to be our very heartbeat.

At this dedication, I didn't realize that they would have each deacon and their family at the front of the church and have them prayed for by the church members. What an amazing blessing to have people one by one by one pray for us. It makes me emotional thinking about the love and support. Our own children (except Bria who lived in Houston by this time) prayed for us.

Sometimes life doesn't happen the way we want it to...we didn't want to take this picture last night, but we have to go back to what we know. God is good no matter where we are...No matter what we are going through...and we praise Him for who He is no matter where we are. He gets the glory for our life NOT Satan. This picture defeats the enemy. He will not win.

My dad came to the hospital because he his heart was racing, he felt sluggish and light headed and felt like he was going to pass out. They have run tests to make sure everything is okay. So far so good! We appreciate your prayers!

"Have I not commanded you? Be strong and courageous. Do not be afraid; do not be discouraged, for the Lord your God will be with you wherever you go.""
Joshua 1:9

#smilingdefeatssatan
#tellingyouaboutitdefeatssatan
#wewinnomatter
#Godisbiggerthanourproblems
#greenwoodstrong

Roosevelt's Reflection:

I talked earlier about anxiety and needing medication to combat the uncontrolled feeling of a desperate situation. On this particular day, I was resting in bed, but I didn't want to be there. Shay was resting with me, and she had fallen asleep. I decided to get up and go to Walmart because I had to pick up something for a project I had going on. As I got out the car I started to feel really funny, sort of like I was walking but I wasn't going anywhere. I proceeded into Walmart and was able to get what I needed, checked out and as I was on my way out of Walmart, I begin to feel as though I was walking on air. I had never experienced this feeling before, and I had not been told by my doctors that this would be a side effect of any of the drugs I was taking. The farther I walked the slower my steps got and my heart started to race uncontrollably. I began to do what I do a lot and that's pray. I began to talk to God and say, "Lord don't let me pass out here in the parking lot of Walmart," just allow me to make it to my car. In order to make it to my car, I had to take baby steps, walking as if I were walking in slow motion. It seemed like it took me forever to get to my car. Thankfully the car was parked closer to the front of the store. I made it to the car, and by this time, I was shaking uncontrollably. As I reached for my phone to dial, my hands were trembling uncontrollably. I was somehow able to dial Shay's number and say, "Shay can you come and pick me up?". I ended up in the emergency room, and after running all the tests they determined that I was fine. We later thought that I had a panic attack, but after further analysis, it was determined that my episode was from me not taking my steroids as prescribed. I am one who feels as though I don't need all the meds that I am prescribed, especially when I feel good. I heard about the opioid crisis in America and I had said to myself, well I feel great, so I don't need this prednisone today. Big mistake. I now take my meds as prescribed!

Shay's Reflection:

I was SO tired in this picture. I was mentally and physically exhausted at this point. I even tear up as I write this because of all of the feelings that come flooding back to me. This part of the journey started earlier in the day. I was taking a nap, which is something that I really never do. Roosevelt was asleep next to me, or so I thought he was. All of a sudden, I woke up to one of the boys passing me the phone and saying, "dad needs you." The conversation went something like:

Me: Hello?

Roosevelt: "I need for you to come and pick me up."

Me: "Pick you up from where? Where are you??

Roosevelt: "I'm in the Walmart parking lot, and I don't feel right."

The conversation is a blur from there. As he was talking, I was rushing to put on my clothes. I hung up and immediately dialed 911. I told them what he said, his phone number, and where he was located. I jumped into the car and sped off. The questions were flooding my mind. Is he having a heart attack? Is he having a really bad anxiety attack? I really didn't know. I live about 3 miles from the interstate, and by the time I got to the interstate, a random number called me. Normally, I wouldn't answer it. But, I picked it up just in case. It was a police officer. She told me to slow down. How in the world did she know? She said, "we are with your husband, and he is okay. We need for you to slow down and take your time getting here. We are taking care of him." I totally lost it! I started crying and told her, " Thank you, thank you so much." I can't remember the order of all of this, but I remember calling Neil, our Executive Pastor and my life group leader at church and I called Roosevelt's step-mom, Ozie. They were my direct connections to get people to pray for Roosevelt. By the time, I got there...I saw Neil and a swarm of police officers around Roosevelt's vehicle. I got out of my car, and they were checking his blood pressure and said he seemed to be okay. His vitals were normal, but his blood pressure seemed high. We went to the hospital.

I'm so thankful for the people who constantly came to the hospital. Some of our journey is a blur. The people are a blur. BUT, I know that we felt loved and cared for, and, it made a difference. Thank you doesn't really cover how we feel about each and every person who prayed, put money in our hand, and came to see us. My prayer is that others feel loved and cared for in their time of need.

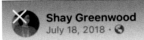

Shay Greenwood
July 18, 2018 · 🌐

I love when God speaks to my heart as I wake up! I just wanted to pass this along to you also...you may need a little encouragement for your day.

"We should be full of faith and full of hope because of our relationship with Jesus Christ. No matter how difficult the circumstances...that's how we are called to walk in this life."

Is that hard? Absolutely. Is it impossible? No.
Let's continue to keep putting one foot in front of the other no matter how crazy life seems. The Holy Spirit gives us the strength to do so. 🖤😌

I'm head to Texas this week without my honey and we are going to be full of faith and full of hope while we are away from each other. This is our story and we are sticking to it. 😒😔 **Roosevelt** hasn't felt well this week (just a part of this journey we are on) and I'm soliciting your prayers as I leave for the next few days that all will be well. Asking for you to pray because I know you will. He's feeling extra tired and extra stressed this week and probably doesn't want me to tell you...BUT that's too bad. We started this journey with you all and we are going to keep fighting through it knowing you are there willing to pray. (and besides Satan is a liar...and I'm bringing him into the light. He loves to isolate us. Has he isolated you?? Call him out today ‼️ Don't let him win. We are praying with you too.)

Pray for hope, strength, and a peace that surpasses all understanding.

I'm reminded of this song....
We have come this far by faith.
Leaning on the Lord
Trusting in His holy word
He's never failed me yet
Can't turn around
He's never failed me yet.

Let's continue to walk by faith and not by sight ‼️🙌🏾📿 I'm encouraging you to walk this way in your life too. We can walk by faith together!!

Roosevelt's Reflection:

For a few days, I felt weak and didn't know what was wrong with me. My last doctor's appointment went well. My energy level started getting lower and lower. I was losing weight, and my frame seemed to be smaller. Shay being my encourager would go through a laundry list of things:

Are you having a hot flash?

Did you eat?

Have you been drinking enough water?

This was her way of helping me to understand that if I missed any of these things then I could do something about it. But, deep down, I knew that it was something different. I managed to gather enough energy to go to the grocery store. While in the grocery store, I felt like I was going to pass out. I was able to get back home. I fell into the bed crying out of frustration and wondering why did I feel so bad. I said to myself, "If this is the way it's going to be, I would rather be with Jesus."

Shay was leaving for Dallas the next day for a business trip. A part of me thought that Shay may think that I was being a little "extra". But, I really wasn't trying to get her to stay home.

In the meantime, I had a tremendous thirst. I had a dry mouth constantly. I purchased apple juice and orange juice not realizing what was going on with me. Even though Shay left, she arranged for me to see the doctor. Chandler was staying at home with me and took me to my appointment. Dr. Qu asked me how I was feeling. I told him that I felt horrible, and he said he was going to check me for diabetes. I told him there was no way I had diabetes. He said he would call me with the results.

He didn't call me. He called Shay and she called Chandler to take me to the hospital because my blood sugar was over 1000. I should have been in a diabetic coma or had a stroke or dead by now. But, God said not so.

Shay's Reflection:

I had a vision that my husband may die that week. I'm just being real. It was so real that I actually texted it to my friends Jan and Chelsey. I told them how horrible Roosevelt was feeling. Roosevelt went to the grocery store and came home feel defeated because he felt so badly. He felt fatigued; he just didn't' feel like himself. He came home, laid across the bed and wept. My first thought was that he knew I was about to go out of town, and he didn't want me to leave. Some days were good...and some days were bad for him up until this point. And, I was in a place where I absolutely needed a break from my life. I love my husband and family. But, I knew I needed a break. However, I had this feeling that something wasn't right, especially when he asked me, "Wonder if something is terribly wrong?" We decided that we would find out at his doctor's appointment the next week. That's when I texted my friends, and they reassured me that everything was going to be okay.

I left for Dallas the next day for a conference for my business. I felt more comfortable knowing that Chandler was at home with the boys with Roosevelt and that he wouldn't be alone. I texted our friend Teri, the hospital doctor, and told her what Roosevelt asked. Teri texted back, "He knows his body. If he thinks something is terribly wrong, he needs to see his doctor." I received that message as I drove to Dallas. I called Dr. Qu and made an appointment for 10. I then called Chandler and told her that dad needed to get dressed and for her to take him to the doctor. After this, things are a blur for me. I know that I received a phone call saying that Roosevelt's blood sugar was at 1000! And, I remember calling home and telling Chandler that she needed to take Roosevelt to the hospital right then. I remember telling her to pack a bag for him. And, I remember my heart breaking. God gave me the feeling that he could die that week and that feeling was true. I was told that when your blood sugar reads 1,000, you should be in a diabetic coma or could suffer from a stroke.

I know you are wondering if I stayed in Dallas. I did. Teri called me and told me that I didn't need to come home. Yes, Roosevelt was going to be in ICU for the week, so I wouldn't be able to stay with him anyway. She promised to take good care of him. And,

Chandler would be with him during the day. I really had a peace about it. It truly was one of those "God will give you a peace that surpasses all understanding" times for me. I knew he was in good hands.

Also, Chandler is a daddy's girl. It was a great chance for her to care for him, and Bria came home from Houston immediately. Everyone stepped up to help their dad. I was grateful that he got the help he needed. I was also able to get a break before the onset of a new illness and the load of information that comes with it.

Chandler Greenwood is with **Roosevelt Greenwood** and **Shay Greenwood**.
July 19, 2018 · 🌐

I posted this on my Instagram yesterday morning. Dad is currently still in the ICU & I'll be able to give a better update later on today. Thank you guys for praying!

·

·

I hear & read all the time about how people don't post enough "real" things on social media, so here's something real:
recently my dad has been suffering with a lot of side effects from all of the medication/treatments he's taking to fight his cancer. currently, my dad feels awful. he's tired. he has no energy. he's overwhelmed. he doesn't have an appetite....and the list goes on. It's real. It's hard. It makes me so sad. It makes us cry. It's hard to watch someone you love so much go through so much pain. my little brother is starting to understand more about what Dad is going through and is becoming more sensitive to it. This is a picture of one way Adam responds when Dad isn't feeling well — he tries to comfort him the best way his sweet little 6 year old self knows how....by giving out the biggest hugs. this picture is so incredibly sweet & it also breaks my heart. knowing that there's nothing we can do to take the cancer away or make our dad feel better in an instant is heartbreaking. with all of that said, to our most amazing &

sweetest prayer warriors, would you guys please pray for my dad that he would feel better soon, side effects would go away, and that the Lord would give him energy and strength! he's also suffering from dry mouth (another side effect from one of his treatments), so please pray for the Lord to relieve him of that too. clinging to the promises that Jesus is

Make Profile Picture

👍 Like   💬 Comment   ↪ Share

Roosevelt's Reflection:

This picture makes we want to weep because I don't have the energy to play with my 6 year old, and although he is not fully aware of what's going on with me his spirit tells him that something is not right. He came and laid with me and said nothing. He just laid his head on my chest. He just wanted me to touch him.

Shay's Reflection:

Sometimes I wonder, does Adam really know what's going on with Roosevelt? We don't really think he knows. He knows when his dad doesn't feel well, but that's about it. I don't think I have even had a conversation with him directly about it. My momma's heart just doesn't want him to have to worry about his dad more than he needs to, and I think it's okay...for now, anyway. I'm sure as he gets older he will ask more questions.

We are so thankful for our children who have stepped up to the plate in every way. Chandler stayed with Roosevelt at the hospital during the day and Bria was with Adam. We had friends and family who brought food every single time we were in the hospital. We felt so blessed by the support and prayers every. single. time.

Shay Greenwood
July 23, 2018 · 🌐

‹ ⋯

Home sweet home ‼️
Thank you for praying. (Magnify this by a million.)
There is no doubt that prayer changes things.
Roosevelt said it today thinking about the goodness of the Lord..."Shay, I know that me being alive is a miracle." He was so sick last week and God spared him going into a diabetic coma or worse.

We now will have a strict diet and insulin 3 times a day. Hard...but we know God will give us the strength and endurance to fight this too. 🙏🏽🕊️

People keep asking what can they do... ‼️

✔️ Order jewelry or find others who love it:
https://premierdesigns.com/ShopForEvent/31018/168526
(If for some reason the site doesn't work, you can message
me pictures of what you want and I can send you an invoice
to pay. Here is the link to the flip catalog: http://
online.pubhtml5.com/ggcg/wkov/)

It's going to take me some time to get back into the swing of
things in making sure Roosevelt is taken care of properly
and this is the help we need right now. And of course,
praying‼️ Ohhhh how we appreciate your prayers!

We love and appreciate all of you so much‼️ 📿 🤍 🖤 🥹
#greenwoodstrong

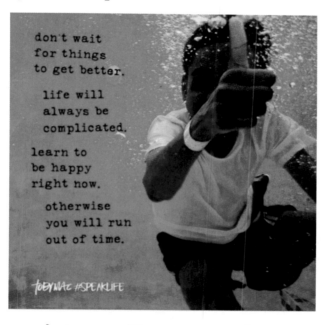

don't wait
for things
to get better.

life will
always be
complicated.

learn to
be happy
right now.

otherwise
you will run
out of time.

TOBYMAC #SPEAKLIFE

👍 Like   💬 Comment   ↪️ Share

👍❤️ **Michelle Mimi Davis and 253 others**

10 shares

Having gone through a diagnosis of stage four cancer and having it be debilitating both physically and mentally and having gone through 25 rounds of radiation and five rounds of chemotherapy, I felt that it must be the worst of it. Not. One day I was walking around the house trying to stay busy by going outside cutting the yard, not wanting to focus on all the issues that I have and why I have those issues, I began to feel overly tired. With chemotherapy and radiation, it takes a lot out of you. It kills cancer cells, but it also kills good cells, so it leaves your body kind of off-line. I said to my wife one day after coming home from the grocery store that I didn't feel right and I wondered if something was terribly wrong. She had already planned to go to Dallas during this time, so me wondering if there was something terribly wrong struck a nerve with her. She called my doctor and got me an appointment just thinking that my meds were having some sort of adverse affect on me. She makes me the appointment and was still able to make her scheduled trip to Dallas. I was visibly weak; I had lost weight. Shay had my daughter, Chandler, to take me to the doctor's appointment. As we go into the doctor's appointment, they do all the tests. I go see the doctor, and the doctor asked me how I was doing. I said to him that I didn't feel great. He looked at me and could tell that I was not doing great. From my blood work, everything looked good, so he didn't understand why I was losing all this weight, feeling so weak and tired. Then he said that I may be dealing with diabetes. Prior to him saying this, I had never heard the word diabetes as it relates to me and my illness, but unbeknownst to me, the medications that I take, steroids, have a negative effect on your body in addition to the positive effect as it relates to the cancer drug that I'm taking. As a negative side effect it could cause your blood sugar to go high. Because I didn't know this, I was walking around with a lot of other issues. He told me that he was going to check my A1C and see what it was. We left the doctor's office, and Chandler drove me home. I got in the bed. I was lying in the bed so weak, and I hear in the background Shay talking to Noah. I hear him saying "yes ma'am, yes ma'am". What should I get? Yes ma'am. I should get how many pieces of clothing? Yes ma'am. Should I get his hat? Yes ma'am." I was lying in bed and I knew that she was having him prepare a bag with my belongings for yet another hospital stay. When I got on the phone with her, she said that my doctor said that I needed to get to the emergency room as quick as I could because my blood sugar was at 1000. Shay called our friends and pastor to let them know what was going on and asked them to pray for me. As I was on the way to the emergency room, my pastor, Rob, called me and asked if there was anything he could do. I said just pray for me and he immediately started to pray. When we got to the emergency room, they ran all the tests, and they said that a normal blood sugar was somewhere between 90 and less than 200, and I was at 1000. He said that most people go into cardiac arrest, stroke, or even a coma at this high of a reading. This was another miracle. I have lost count of how many miracles that have actually taken place in my life during the series of events that started with me being diagnosed with stage four cancer, but this was another miracle that God afforded me. They admitted me to the hospital and put me in ICU. I stayed in the ICU for about three days. My wife was in Dallas, but my children were there, and they were taking really good care of me. By this time, I was really in my feelings. Big time. I now had this issue on top of the diagnosis of stage four cancer and all of the medications that I'm already taking to now have to deal with having to possibly take more medication for another issue. Visitors to came to see me in the ICU. I asked Pastor Rob if he thought that I was being punished for something. He said no. My stay was about a week in the ICU, and I thank God that he allowed me to walk into the emergency room and walk out of the emergency room. When I was home, I had to inject insulin into my stomach three times a day to keep my blood sugar normal. I wondered if I could do all of this. I was taking chemo drugs, getting hormone shots, my blood pressure out of whack, and on top of all of that, I had to take insulin. I was in a pretty bad way, but in all of that, I was still positive. My wife had done all the research, and men who have my diagnosis take pain meds because the pain is uncontrollable. I always try to see the good in the bad, and although I was taking a lot of different medications, I could still go about and be productive during the day. I was in no pain at all 90 percent of the time, whereas when I was first diagnosed, I was taking two morphine pills, Percocet, and one Valium because those were the only things that would stop the pain. I count that as a win and I have to count all of the small battles and just believe that I'm going to win the war.

Shay's Reflection:

It breaks my heart when I think about all that Roosevelt has had to go through. Why does his body fail him?? At this time, it was mostly because of the side effects from the medicine he was on. Type 2 Diabetes is better to treat than not taking his chemo pill with the steroid and have the cancer cells come back. No way do we want that. Earlier after his diagnosis, Roosevelt took the genetic test to see if he was born with the cancer gene, and he tested negative. We may never know why his cells formed cancer cells in his prostate so aggressively at such a young age. It was hard to watch him be so sick with a new illness. I was so incredibly thankful that God spared his life once again.

<  **Shay Greenwood**
August 31, 2018 · 🌐 ···

Woke up thinking about what **Roosevelt Greenwood**'s doctor said to us Wednesday... that if we would have waited just a week more to take him to the hospital this last time....he would have died. Then, my mind went to the Nurse Practitioner asking Roosevelt if he had any bone pain...."No" was his answer.

Glory to God! 🙌 He's a walking miracle.
I can't get over what God has done.
It's the power of ALL of us praying.
Thank you!
A 1000 glucose reading...to now regularly around 100.
Stage 4 Metastatic prostate cancer diagnosis that began with HORRENDOUS spine pain where he could barely walk...initially he was on two Morphine pills a day, Percocet for break-thru pain and a Valium at night to NO pain pills NOW - at all - ever!!!

We should never doubt the power of prayer. 🙌
Does it always happen the way we want.
Nope.
But we can see what God has done in every situation! He's
good always.
Let's count the ways...
Share below your testimony of the power of prayer in your
life....even the little things matter.
#Godisatworkineverysituation #greenwoodstrong

👍 Like   💬 Comment   ↪ Share

👍😲 **Jody Fayman and 457 others**

6 shares

Roosevelt's Reflection:

On this journey, you can't do it by yourself. Someone
once said that when fear comes knocking, let faith
answer the door. My faith has really been put to the
test. I don't know what my future holds, but I know

Who holds my future, If you are thinking about giving up, don't. Keep fighting, and when you can't fight any longer, let your love ones fight for you.

Shay's Reflection:

As we think about what we have been through over the past three years, one of the best decisions that we made in the beginning was to ask for prayer. We didn't really think through how it would impact every step in this journey. We had so many people praying for Roosevelt's healing and provision for our family. Every step, we asked for prayer from close friends and family and from our life group and Church. I was completely overwhelmed by everything; I couldn't make it on my own. There were times where my life and the circumstances felt so heavy that I didn't have the words to pray. It was so comforting to know that I had friends and family whom I could call on to hold the bucket when I needed to vent my frustration and pray for us when I needed them.

Prayers were answered in so many ways during this journey. God also provided for our needs in every way.

We found out recently that when Dr. Qu first saw Roosevelt and his initial diagnosis, he gave him eighteen months to two years to live. We couldn't believe it. We intentionally chose Dr. Qu because he had a reputation for being upfront and honest. If you had 6 months to live, he would tell you. I remember vividly asking Dr. Qu initially what he thought, and God didn't allow him to tell us. We still can't believe that's what his prognosis was, and we didn't know.

Bria, our oldest, who received a spot on a professional contemporary dance company in Houston, said that she wouldn't have moved to Houston if she would have known that. We are thankful for how God gives us the information we need to live out His will for our lives. It will be three years in September 2019, and Roosevelt's PSA has been undetectable since November 2016, a great indication that prayer changes things.

I could cry about how the Lord has worked out our insurance issues along the way. I remember crying when Roosevelt's insurance went from our Affordable Care Act policy, better know as Obama Care, to Medicare. It was so distressing to feel like we started from scratch. I felt like I was learning a foreign language, and honestly, I wasn't up to learning another. But, I had to. I had friends praying for us during this time and watched how God not only placed people in our path to help me choose the best way to go, but God also provided the money we needed for the Medicare Supplement policy. Every time we went through something new, it really strengthened our faith about how God cares and supplies our every need.

Where are we now?

We are praising God today and everyday! Three years ago, Roosevelt Greenwood was diagnosed with Stage 4 Metastatic Prostate Cancer- September 7, 2016. They told us that it was a chronic diagnosis...with no cure. His PSA was 1,490. The normal range is 0 to 4.

Roosevelt was in so much pain in his back that he had to take an enormous amount of pain medicine - which meant he couldn't drive and was always lethargic. We were devastated and dreams for the life we had hoped for were shattered.

But God⏸️ Roosevelt believed that he would win no matter what - alive here on earth, or alive with Jesus in heaven. Right now, he is here on earth and we are SO thankful and have seen miracle after miracle happen in his life. To God Be the glory for what He has done!

Roosevelt has no pain now - ever. His PSA has been undetectable - less than 1 - since March 2017 because of various treatments. He takes 4 chemo pills a day, takes a monthly hormone shot and bone shot, and manages type 2 diabetes (which was caused by steroids). Generally, he feels good now that we have figured out how to manage everything. He has changed his diet and exercises regularly either by walking or mowing the lawn. It's not easy at all. It's a new normal life.

We went walking this morning. As we walked, we listened to a song called "He has His hands on you" by Marvin Sapp. It's hard, but we are determined to count our blessings rather than our losses. The enemy of our lives would like us to focus on what's wrong rather than what's right. We aren't in denial. We deal with reality. We just don't want to waste so much time focusing on the things we can't control. (We have found personally that it leads to constant sadness, depression, overwhelm, fear, stress - and it doesn't change our situations.)

None of us knows how many days we have to live on earth with our loved ones. We praise God for the days

He is providing. We give Him glory and honor for what He is doing in Roosevelt's life right now. We will never take it for granted because it could be so different!!
We are so thankful for all of you and your constant encouragement and support!!

The words to that song which encouraged us this morning are listed here...
Maybe you need them too??

_____

He Has His Hands On You - Marvin Sapp

_____

He sees the tears you cry
He shares your pain inside
And sometimes you wonder why
He allows you to go through what you go through
just know He has His hands on you
your days are filled with dark clouds
even when the sun is out
and from the top of your lungs
You shout, will there ever be a change, what shall I do?
Just know He has His hands on you
He has His hands on you
He says He'll see you through
When you cry, He's holding you
So just lift your hands up high
For He will provide
Just know He has His hands on you
Sometimes you feel so alone
Like a child lost with no home
They keep telling you to be strong
But you...

Made in the USA
Lexington, KY
17 November 2019